CORPORATE DEVIANCE

D1373899

M. DAVID ERMANN
University of Delaware

RICHARD J. LUNDMAN
The Ohio State University

HOLT, RINEHART AND WINSTON

New York   Chicago   San   Francisco   Philadelphia
Montreal   Toronto   London   Sydney   Tokyo   Mexico City
Rio de Janeiro   Madrid

Library of Congress Cataloging in Publication Data

Ermann, M. David.
    Corporate deviance.

    Bibliography: p.
    Includes index.
    1. White collar crimes. 2. Corporations--Corrupt
practices. I. Lundman, Richard J., 1944-   .
II. Title.
HV6768.E75   364.1'68   81-6849
                                             AACR2

ISBN: 0-03-044386-5

CBS COLLEGE PUBLISHING
Holt, Rinehart and Winston
The Dryden Press
Saunders College Publishing

To

Marlene, Michael, and Natalie Ermann

and

Jean, Bobby, and Julie Lundman

PREFACE

This book is about the fact that people, acting collectively in corporations, sometimes break rules or laws and can be labeled deviant. It develops an organizationally sensitive analysis of deviance in those instances where large corporations are the appropriate units of analysis, while typically no one person is labeled deviant. Such a perspective is unavoidable when analyzing events such as the knowing exposure of employees to workplace hazards, or the patently illegal contributions made for many years by many corporations to important political figures.

Our goal is to apply current research on deviance to the study of organizations, and current understandings of organizational behavior to the study of deviance. We expand the study of deviance by including the large corporation, a type of social actor only infrequently encountered in existing analyses of deviance, and we expand the study of complex organizations by introducing a systematic concern for their deviant outputs.[1] Our twin objectives are to understand both the external forces that accompany public labeling of corporate acts as deviant, and the internal administrative patterns that result in behaviors publicly labeled as deviant.

While recognizing the complexities of the organizational and deviance perspectives, we have tried to write with a style, clarity, and pace appropriate for students in deviance, social problems, criminology, organizations, and business and society courses. The first two chapters analyze the nature of corporate acts and the processes by which they are defined as deviant. The next four chapters analyze types of deviant corporate acts and develop in-depth case studies of deception of stockholders, creation of work-related illnesses and deaths, price-fixing, and funneling of corporate funds to politicians. The final two chapters describe and evaluate alternative strategies for the control of corporate deviance. To facilitate student research, each chapter contains a selective annotated bibliography, and an appendix contains an extensive unannotated bibliography.

ACKNOWLEDGMENTS

We thank William Chambliss, Jeffrey Davidson, Carl Klockars, Ronald Martin, Robert Meier, James Short, Jr., Neal Shover, Christopher Stone,

[1]Sherman correctly argues that "theories of organizations . . . have been largely concerned with the structural and other internal properties of organizations rather than with their outputs generally." See Lawrence R. Sherman, "A Theoretical Strategy for Organizational Deviance," unpublished paper, Criminal Justice Research Center, SUNY, Albany, New York, 1980, p. 1.

and William Waegel for the suggestions and criticisms they advanced after reading various earlier versions of this book. They contributed numerous insights and suggested changes to correct our oversights and excesses.

Our secretaries often went well beyond the responsibilities of office to help us. For their excellent work and for their help in making those deadlines we did meet, we thank Carol Anderson, Claire Blessing, Marie Gregg, Pat Bunville, and Eileen Prybolski at Delaware, and Cindy Brown, Marsha Nicol, and Laurie Taress at Ohio State. We are extremely appreciative.

For their help in a variety of important ways as research assistants, we thank Brenda Wixon Donnelly, Donald Berry, and Marcia Block. We also thank the Center for Science and Culture at Delaware for support that aided Dave Ermann as the book neared completion. And for their conscientious work on our behalf at Holt, Rinehart and Winston, we thank Frank Graham, Patrick Powers, Elyse Brookstein, and Brian Heald.

We also thank our families, Marlene, Michael, and Natalie Ermann, and Jean, Bobby, and Julie Lundman for support and patience that occasionally bordered on the heroic. We thank them for the evenings, the weekends, and, especially, that long week in June when we worked on the production copy of the book.

This book is the joint product of the authors. We shared equally in its creation as all parts of it were discussed, exchanged, and rewritten innumerable times. The order of our names merely is alphabetical.

M.D.E.   R.J.L.
Newark, Delaware   Worthington, Ohio

INSTRUCTORS' INTRODUCTION

This brief introduction is designed to give instructors a summary of the social science perspectives we have adopted in this book.

Corporate deviance originates in complex organizational settings composed of subunits more loosely tied to one another than is usually imagined.[1] Each subunit's unstated goals and standard procedures often only vaguely relate to the overall stated goals of the corporation. Deviant corporate actions therefore are seldom produced by single-minded commitments to financial gain, compelling the corporation to violate norms whenever rationally calculated corporate interests indicate that profits for stockholders would be increased. Corporations are not such simple organisms.

Rather, corporate deviance typically occurs in an environment in which the subunits of a corporation are pursuing their own interests and people are just doing their jobs. The selling of the dangerous Pinto by Ford, for example, flowed from the interplay of competing managerial coalitions at Ford, not from a rational profit-seeking decision of one individual or of a monolithic organization. The complex organizational structure at Ford in turn reflected in part the tendencies of all large organizations and in part the history and external pressures experienced by this particular company.

However, actions such as Ford's are not intrinsically deviant. Just as Howard S. Becker and others[2] directed attention to the question of how rules for individual behavior are created and enforced, we propose that these questions must now be asked of organizations. Sociologists must study the external forces that define or fail to define specific corporate acts as deviant.

In particular, it appears that for a corporation and its behaviors a label of deviance results from social processes of rule creation and rule enforcement. First, some individuals or organizations accuse the corporation of an act that they perceive as deviant. In response, the corporation typically resists these accusations by "stonewalling," attacking the motives or competence of its accusers, or enhancing its identity as a socially responsible entity.[3] Witnessing this process of give-and-take is an audience that includes branches of government, consumers, and potential plaintiffs, and that evaluates the accusations and defenses and occasionally applies negative sanctions to the corporation. As a result of this process, corporations and their actions at some times and in some places come to be defined as deviant.

We organize this process in terms of a *cui bono* (who benefits?) perspective, first used in our paper on organizational deviance and its control.[4] This perspective suggests that for an act to be deviant, it must be defined and responded to as violating the rights of a group of actors in contact with the corporation. The various categories (owners, employees, customers, and public-at-large) are each held to have different rights. Because there are different categories of actors with different rights that are socially defined and frequently changing, there are different types of deviance based on whose rights to what benefits are held to be violated at any particular moment.

Our goal thus is to portray the texture and dynamics whereby internal organizational processes and their consequences can be labeled deviant. We trace the inner histories of corporate actions, and the external social histories of how such acts can come to be defined as deviant. Our approach is eclectic because no single analysis now available fits the data sufficiently well. Our explanations therefore draw from a variety of perspectives within sociology and from other disciplines as well.

SOME EXCLUSIONS

This book is about corporations and not about other large organizations. We originally planned to include many forms of organizations because of similarities in their organizational behaviors and their external environments. The basic structure would have been the same as the present one is, and in fact much noncorporate material was written and then set aside when we realized that the manuscript was becoming too long and complicated for its teaching purposes. We believe, however, that the basic insights presented here are generally applicable to noncorporate organizations, and we each have written elsewhere about these other organizations.[5]

Second, this book is not about all corporations, but is limited to corporations as they exist in the United States. This is largely a matter of necessity. Data and especially theory for even this limited topic are still sparse, so we have chosen not to complicate our presentation with necessarily tentative crosscultural comparisons. We believe, however, that comparative study will prove useful as descriptive and analytical resources improve. Much insight would probably result, for example, from directly comparing socially defined deviance against employees in socialist and in capitalist societies.

Third, this book is not an exposé in the spirit of consumer advocate Ralph Nader[6] and others.[7] Such efforts serve important purposes by generating public awareness of harmful corporate actions. But they are typically rich in description and limited in analysis. We seek instead to use and enrich the organizational and deviance perspectives as they currently exist within sociology.

Nevertheless, the biases and sometimes the anger evident in works primarily intended to generate public awareness are present in this book. We know ourselves to be particularly bothered by those corporate acts that affect large numbers of people, cause physical rather than limited financial harm, or are intentional or predictable rather than reasonably unanticipated. These and other biases may make our analysis offensive to some.

Finally, this is not a book about white-collar crime. "Corporate deviance" and "white-collar crime" are not synonyms. Edwin Sutherland coined the latter term and used it well through a series of papers and a subsequent book with that title published in 1949.[8] Beginning in the 1960s, however, Sutherland's definition was frequently criticized, primarily for being too inclusive.[9] Its use complicates the study of some already complicated phenomena because there is little but collar color that unites fraud, embezzlement, pollution, and price-fixing. The term is in most regards not a single concept. For this reason, alternative concepts must be created by breaking down and reorganizing the elements of white-collar crime and adding other elements. Corporate deviance, we believe, is one such concept because it allows the economical study of theoretically related actions. By focusing exclusively on socially disapproved actions of large organizations, it gains some of the insights already developed in the study of deviance and of organizations.

In sum, we are addressing two types of questions: Why do corporations act in deviant ways, and why are these actions considered deviant? Sociologists must avoid the temptation to mystify or sidestep these questions. It is all too easy to treat corporations as simplified and unitary black boxes that inherently produce deviance, or to ignore entirely the issue of social reaction to corporate actions. This book addresses both of these issues.

NOTES

1. Karl E. Weick, "Educational Organizations as Loosely Coupled Systems," *Administrative Science Quarterly* 21 (1976): 1–19.
2. Howard S. Becker, *Outsiders: Studies in the Sociology of Deviance* (New York: Free Press, 1963); Erich Goode, *Deviance Behavior: An Interactionist Approach* (Englewood Cliffs, N.J.: Prentice-Hall, 1978).
3. See William Waegel, M. David Ermann, and Alan M. Horowitz, "Organizational Responses to Imputations of Deviance," *The Sociological Quarterly*, forthcoming.

4. M. David Ermann and Richard J. Lundman, "Deviant Acts by Complex Organizations: Deviance and Social Control at the Organizational Level of Analysis," *The Sociological Quarterly* 19 (1978); 55–67.

5. Waegel, Ermann, and Horowitz, "Organizational Responses"; M. David Ermann, "The Social Control of Organizations in the Health Care Area," *Milbank Memorial Fund Quarterly—Health and Society* 54 (1976): 167–183; Richard J. Lundman, "Organizational Norms and Police Discretion: An Observational Study of Police Work with Traffic Law Violators," *Criminology* 17 (August 1979): 159–171; Richard J. Lundman, *Police and Policing: An Introduction* (New York: Holt, Rinehart and Winston, 1980), pp. 137–168.

6. For example, Ralph Nader, *Unsafe at Any Speed: The Designed-in Dangers of the American Automobile* (New York: Grossman 1965).

7. David Boulton, *The Grease Machine: The Inside Story of Lockheed's Dollar Diplomacy* (New York: Harper & Row, 1978); J. Patrick Wright, *On a Clear Day You Can See General Motors: John Z. Delorean's Look inside the Automotive Giant* (Grosse Pointe, Michigan: Wright Enterprises, 1979).

8. Edwin H. Sutherland, *White-Collar Crime* (New York: Holt, Rinehart and Winston, 1949).

9. For example, Earl R. Quinney, "The Study of White Collar Crime: Toward a Reorientation in Theory and Research," *Journal of Criminal Law, Criminology and Police Science* 55 (1964): 208–214.

CONTENTS

Contents

ONE

The corporate deviance framework

1

Corporate acts

When a new member enters the organization, he [or she] is confronted with a social structure . . . and a set of expectations for . . . behavior. It does not matter who the particular individual is; the organization has established a system of norms and expectations to be followed regardless of who its personnel happen to be, and it continues to exist regardless of personnel turnover.

—*Richard H. Hall*[1]

This book is about corporate deviance. It describes the origins of corporate acts and shows how these acts sometimes are labeled deviant. It analyzes types of deviant corporate acts and reviews various attempts at control. Throughout, it emphasizes the analytical importance of corporate bureaucratic organization.

Consider the problem of work-related employee deaths. It has been argued that the vast majority of the 100,000 annual employee deaths from work-related illnesses[2] are avoidable by using existing technology.[3] Some forms of cancer, for example, have been known to be caused by certain working conditions for more than two hundred years. In 1775 an English surgeon, Sir Percival Pott, reported a high rate of scrotal cancer among London chimney sweeps. "Yet, today, thousands of coke oven workers in the United States are exposed to the same kind of coal combination by-products—and those with the heaviest exposures are dying ... at a rate of ten times higher than that of other steelworkers."[4] Such unnecessary deaths have long been known and continue to occur in many other work settings:

> Some 130 years after the discovery of scrotal cancer among copper smelters exposed to inorganic arsenic, 1.5 million American workers still are exposed to arsenic. According to recent reports, some of them are dying of lung and lymphatic cancers at two to eight times the national rate.
>
> In 1973, 80 years after aromatic amines were found to cause bladder cancer among German dye workers, thousands of American workers were still literally sloshing in them. Fifty percent of former employees at one benzidine plant have developed bladder cancer.[5]

These avoidable work-related deaths are products of the corporate contexts in which they occur. Just as violence by members of adolescent gangs cannot be explained without reference to the structure and functioning of the gang, harm to workers cannot be explained without reference to corporate structure and functioning. It is not their upbringing that makes executives act as they do. They probably never would knowingly expose their family, friends, or neighbors to similar levels of risk. Rather, it is in their positions within corporate bureaucratic organizations that executives produce avoidable deaths.

CORPORATE BUREAUCRATIC ORGANIZATION

Max Weber's concept of "bureaucracy"[6] contains several ideas that are useful in establishing the organizational origins of corporate deviance. As described by Weber, a bureaucracy consists of a large number of positions. These positions relate to one another hierarchically and form a pyramid as people in particular positions report to a smaller number of people in higher-level positions. We first will discuss the nature of positions in corporate organizations. Then we will expand upon Weber's description of hierarchical relations by adding the idea of administrative coalitions.

Corporate Positions

The corporation can be viewed as "a collection of jobs or social positions, each with its own skills, powers, rules, and rewards."[7] These social positions include personnel recruiters, public relations representatives, salespeople, laborers, secretaries, and vice-presidents. Together with other positions, they are the building blocks of large corporations. Personnel recruiters attempt to find new employees, public relations representatives try to put the best face on corporate acts, and sales personnel try to keep customers coming back. Collectively, these positions influence what the corporation produces, whether it survives, and how it changes.

Corporations and other organizations thus are not mere collections of people. Rather, they are collections of positions. The organization and its positions are stable at least in the short run and may continue indefinitely, even though all its people eventually are replaced.

Consider a possibly familiar example: universities and two positions within them, students and instructors. Although some of us may want to resist the idea, particular people are not the main determiners of most actions within this setting. Most of what students and professors do is the result of formal and informal definitions and powers associated with the social positions they occupy. This is why similarities among American universities are greater than differences, courses taken at one university are readily transferable to most others, and a person who was a teacher or student at one will have few surprises moving to another.

There are differences between individuals in university settings, of course, with some professors more interesting and some students more attentive. But the positions of student and professor are indispensable for understanding the organization. Other people could easily enact the basic student and instructor roles. If all its people were replaced, the university's functioning would not change dramatically. In fact, this is exactly what happens as students graduate and professors are replaced on a regular basis. They come and go, but the organization persists.

Similar cycles occur in corporations. Workers, managers, and elites are replaced regularly. This turnover is not threatening to the corporation because recruitment of replacements typically is well organized. People tend to have corporate careers lasting many years, adding to their training as they move through a series of positions. They draw on their past experiences and quickly learn what is expected in new positions by using the files, the formal rules and written job descriptions, and the informal expectations they pick up in the course of their work. Except in unusual cases, they come and go in an orderly fashion while the corporation continues with surprisingly few changes.

Of course, people sometimes do not conform so neatly to the requirements of their corporate positions. People bring aspirations, beliefs, abilities, and needs to their jobs. Therefore there can be poor fits between the requirements of a position and the traits of its occupant. In the cases of corporate deviance studied for this book, however, these situations appear to be rare.

The corporation thus is real because most people mold themselves to their corporate positions most of the time. Corporate positions are separate from, and usually more important than, the people who hold them.

Administrative Coalitions

According to organization charts, corporate positions relate to one another hierarchically. Each position is under the supervision of a higher one. The single occupant of the top position, therefore, would seem to be the person who determines which corporate acts will happen.

Corporate reality is more complex, however. Corporate presidents do make decisions, but their time, interests, and skills are too limited for them to make or even participate in every important decision. Hence, corporate acts rarely are the result of the unilateral decision of a corporate president.[8]

Corporate acts instead are the result of decisions made by a constantly shifting series of administrative coalitions.[9] Engineers, plant managers, accountants, and public relations experts may work together to devise a corporate response to federally mandated pollution standards. Meanwhile, the vice-presidents for marketing and personnel may never know of the discussion or participate in the decision. On other occasions, as with pricing decisions, marketing, legal, and accounting personnel as well as the corporate president may devise a solution in the absence of engineers, plant managers, and public relations representatives. Although corporate presidents participate in some decisions, most of the actions of large corporations are the results of decisions made by administrative coalitions.

CORPORATE ACTS

Corporate positions and coalitions can combine to produce corporate acts in at least three ways. First, the complexity of positions within large corporations can produce an act. Second, corporate elites can indirectly influence actions by establishing particular norms, rewards, and punishments for people occupying lower-level positions. Third, a coalition at or near the top of a corporation can consciously initiate a behavior and explicitly use hierarchically linked positions to implement it.

Acts Traceable to the Complexity of Corporate Positions

People occupying positions within large corporations typically have limited responsibility and information. They are expected to attend to their job and be sensitive to the direction of their corporate superiors. They are not encouraged to look beyond their work-related expectations or rewarded for undertaking actions that are independent of the direction of supervisors.

In this typical situation it is possible for people in corporate positions to do their jobs well and still produce a deviant action. This is because no one person has the responsibility, incentive, time, or skill to collect, assimilate, and use information needed to coordinate and evaluate corporate actions. Writing before the Three Mile Island nuclear accident, law professor Christopher Stone suggested a hypothetical example of how the complexity of corporate positions might result in a corporate act:

> Suppose, for example, the case of an electric utility company that maintains a nuclear power plant. We can readily imagine that there might be knowledge of physics, evidence of radiation leakage, information regarding temperature variations, data related to previous operation runs in this and other plants, which, if gathered in the mind of one single person, would make his [or her] continued operation of that plant, without a shutdown, wanton and reckless—that is, if an explosion resulted, strong civil and criminal liability could and would be brought to bear on him [or her]. . . . But let us suppose what is more likely to be the case in modern corporate America: that the information and acts are distributed among many different employees engaged in various functional groups within the corporation. The nuclear engineer can be charged with a bit of information a, the architect knows b, the night watchman knows c, the research scientist task force knows d. Conceivably there will not be any

single individual who has ... such knowledge and intent as will support
a charge against him [or her] individually.[10]

Acts Indirectly Traceable to Corporate Elites

Other corporate acts are less a product of complexity, more the inciden-
tal and unintended result of elite initiative. Large corporations regularly confront opportunities and problems with administrative
coalitions emerging in response. These coalitions establish particular
goals, develop operating rules and procedures, and delegate day-to-day
responsibilities to their subordinates. Occasionally, these routine procedures produce unintended results.

For instance: in the late 1960s Ford executive Lee Iacocca and his
allies lobbied within the company for building a small fuel-efficient car
to compete with foreign imports.[11] Eventually, Mr. Iacocca became
Ford president, and his coalition pushed through a crash plan to build
the Pinto in two-thirds the time normally required. As a result, tooling
had to be done simultaneously with design and testing. By the time a
fuel tank safety design problem was discovered, tooling was well under-
way. Nobody would take the problem to corporate elites because, in the
words of one engineer, "Safety wasn't a popular subject around Ford
in those days."[12] Additionally, Mr. Iacocca had an inflexible rule that
the Pinto was not to weigh an ounce over 2,000 pounds or cost a penny
over $2,000. "So, even when a crash test showed that the one pound,
one dollar piece of metal stopped the puncture of the gas tank, it was
thrown out as extra cost and extra weight."[13] The car was sold with the
fuel tank safety design problem.

Nobody in Mr. Iacocca's coalition ordered a car that was unsafe. They
established a goal, developed operating rules, and delegated responsibility to others. The unintended result was an unsafe product.

Acts Directly Traceable to Corporate Elites

However, not all corporate actions are accidents in the sense implied
by Professor Stone or unintentional as illustrated by the Pinto episode.
Corporate elites sometimes undertake actions intended to produce particular results and use corporate positions and hierarchy to achieve
their goals.

In 1959, for instance, four of the Gulf Oil Corporation's top executives—chair and chief operating officer, executive vice-president, comptroller, and general counsel—formed a coalition in response to a
perceived problem: excessive and unfair government interference in
corporate affairs.[14] After a period of deliberation the four decided to

attempt to remedy the problem by making illegal corporate contributions to campaigning and incumbent politicians. Having made this decision they directed others to carry out their initiative.

In forming this coalition and devising a solution, these four executives acted carefully. Members of Gulf's founding family, the Mellons, were not alerted because it was believed they would be opposed. Additionally, others occupying top-level positions also were not informed, either because the perceived problem and emergent solution were not part of their corporate responsibilities or because, as in the case of the Mellons, it was felt they could not be trusted. Last, the occupants of lower-level positions who actually carried out these actions generally were given very little information. They were told what to do and did what they were told.

SUMMARY

In this chapter we presented the first half of a corporate deviance framework. We showed that corporations are structures composed of positions and described the importance of administrative coalitions in corporate hierarchies. We then illustrated some of the ways corporate positions and administrative coalitions produce corporate acts.

Chapter 2 completes the corporate deviance framework by showing how corporate acts occasionally are labeled deviant.

ANNOTATED SELECTED READINGS

Bruyn, Severyn T. *The Social Economy.* New York: Wiley, 1977. Chapter 2 outlines the competing models of what a corporation is and relates these models to the social organization of the economy.

Coleman, James S. *Power and the Structure of Society.* New York: Norton, 1974. An analysis that argues that individuals are marginal in large organizations and that organizations themselves have power.

Ermann, M. David, and Richard J. Lundman. "Deviant Acts by Complex Organizations." *The Sociological Quarterly* 19 (Winter 1978): 55–67. A review of sociological calls for the study of organizational deviance and an anticipation of a conceptual framework.

Gross, Edward. "Organizational Crime: A Theoretical Perspective." *Studies in Symbolic Interaction* 1 (1978). Greenwich, CT: JAI Press. Pp. 55–85. An analysis of why organizational settings, structures, and recruitment make all organizations inherently criminogenic.

Kanter, Rosabeth Moss. *Men and Women of the Corporation.* New York: Basic Books, 1977. A richly detailed and exceptionally well-written account of life within a major corporation.

Mills, C. Wright. *The Power Elite.* New York: Oxford U. P., 1956. One of the best early statements of the nature of elite and institutional power in postindustrial society.

Reiss, Albert J., Jr. "The Study of Deviant Behavior: Where the Action is." *Ohio Valley Sociologist* 32 (Autumn 1966): 60–66. One of the first systematic discussions of the concept of "organizational deviance."

Schrager, Laura Shill, and James F. Short, Jr. "Toward a Sociology of Organizational Crime." *Social Problems* 25:4 (1978): 407–419. Defines organizational crimes in a manner akin to this book and discusses related issues.

NOTES

1. Richard H. Hall, *Organizations: Structure and Process,* 2d ed. (Englewood Cliffs, NJ: Prentice-Hall, 1977), p. 26.

2. *The President's Report on Occupational Safety and Health* (Washington, D.C.: U.S. Government Printing Office, 1973), p. 11.

3. Biophysicist Joel Swartz goes so far as to assert that "the technology exists which could reduce the exposures to all hazardous substances to safe levels or to eliminate them entirely." See his "Silent Killers at Work," *Crime and Social Justice* 3 (Summer 1975): 15.

4. Phyllis Lehmann, "Occupational Cancer," *Job Safety & Health* 3 (July 1975): 5.

5. Ibid., p. 5.

6. The term *bureaucracy* is used here in its sociological sense, not in its everyday sense of bungling, inefficiency, and heavy-handedness. For a description and thorough discussion of the concept, see Peter M. Blau and Marshall W. Meyer, *Bureaucracy in Modern Society,* 2d ed. (New York: Random House, 1971).

7. Jerald Hage and Michael Aiken, *Social Change in Complex Organizations* (New York: Random House, 1970), p. 11. For further discussion of the reality of organizations and the importance of positions, see Hall, *Organizations,* pp. 23–27; Daniel Katz and Robert L. Kahn, *The Social Psychology of Organizations* (New York: Wiley, 1966), pp. 37–38, 48–55, 172–198; and Cyril Sofer, *Organizations in Theory and Practice* (New York: Basic Books, 1972), pp. 220–222.

8. See the discussion of technostructures throughout John Kenneth Galbraith, *The New Industrial State* (New York: New American Library, 1967).

9. For further discussion of administrative coalitions, see James D. Thompson, *Organizations in Action* (New York: McGraw-Hill, 1967). Also see Rosabeth Moss Kanter, *Men and Women of the Corporation* (New York: Basic Books, 1977), pp. 4 ff; Joseph L. Bower, "On the Amoral Organization," in Robin Marris, ed., *The Corporate Society* (New York: Wiley, 1974), pp. 182 ff.

10. Christopher Stone, *Where the Law Ends: Social Control of Corporate Behavior* (New York: Harper & Row, 1975), pp. 51–52.

11. Materials for this discussion of the Pinto are primarily from Mark Dowie, "Pinto Madness," in Jerome H. Skolnich and Elliott Currie, eds., *Crisis in American Institutions,* 4th ed. (Boston: Little, Brown, 1979), pp. 23–41.

12. Ibid., p. 27.

13. Ibid., p. 28.

14. For a brief discussion of this case, see John Brooks, "The Bagman," in Rosabeth Moss Kanter and Barry A. Stein, eds., *Life in Organizations: Workplaces as People Experience Them* (New York: Basic Books, 1979), pp. 363–372. For a more detailed discussion, see Chapter 6 of this book.

Deviant corporate acts

For deviance to become a social fact, somebody must perceive an act, situation, or event as a departure from social norms, must categorize that perception, must report that perception to others, must get them to accept this definition of the situation, and must obtain a response that conforms to their definition. Unless all these requirements are met, deviance as a social fact does not come into being.

—*Earl Rubington and Martin S. Weinberg*[1]

porations greatly influence life in the United States, Canada, and similar societies. In the United States, twenty-five million individuals are owners of corporate stock.[2] Sixteen million are employees of the 500 largest industrial firms,[3] and millions more work for suppliers of these corporations. Everyone is a corporate customer, with 1979 sales by the 500 largest industrials hitting $1.4 trillion.[4] And everyone is a member of the general public affected by corporate decisions on issues ranging from environmental quality to political contributions.

Because corporations are so influential, tradition and law combine to create normative standards for corporate behaviors towards stockholders, employees, customers, and the general public. Stockholders, for example, are held to be entitled to accurate financial information in a limited number of clearly specified areas. And employees are said to have a right to work environments free of known or knowable hazards.

However, these groups frequently feel that their rights have been violated. Customers complain that they have been sold overpriced products. Neighbors publicly worry about corporate dumping of dangerous corporate wastes. In these and other cases, organizations and people come away from their corporate contacts contending that their legitimate interests have been harmed.

Preview of the Chapter

The purpose of this chapter is to describe how corporate acts occasionally are labeled deviant. First we will describe how accusers, accused corporations, and audiences are involved in the corporate deviance-defining process. Then we will discuss the complexities of this process. Finally, we will propose that a deviant label can result from violating the rights of owners, employees, customers, or the public-at-large.

THE CORPORATE DEVIANCE-DEFINING PROCESS

Individuals or groups sometimes feel that their treatment by corporations is a violation of normative standards. In such cases, one option is to terminate contact with the offending corporation.[5] Suspicious pension funds can sell their shares of stock. Worried employees can find other places of employment that seem safer. Customers can search for markets wherein price-fixing is infrequent or nonexistent. And affluent members of the general public can move away from corporate polluters.

The act of breaking contact itself can draw attention to corporate behaviors. For example, the fact that a pension fund is selling its shares in a particular corporation or that important corporate employees have resigned can draw attention to the alleged deviance of a corporation. Whether or not they are intended to do so, these terminations can produce or support accusations of deviance.

Sometimes, however, terminating contact is difficult or undesirable. Pride, prospects of personal or financial loss, and legal constraints are among the factors that make withdrawal unavailable. Some of those who maintain their contact or others who are their allies may then try to direct public attention to perceived corporate departures from normative standards. Angry individual stockholders may try to use proxy statements to mobilize others, or concerned church groups that own stock may use ritualistic annual stockholder meetings as forums for their dissatisfaction. Similarly, neighborhood organizations may attack corporate polluters by pressuring local media for attention or lobbying state and federal legislatures for relief.

Corporations do not remain idle in the face of such efforts to label their actions deviant. Some provide alternative corporate data and interpretations, or they hire sophisticated law or public relations firms. Others engage in elaborate advertising campaigns to improve their images, "stonewall" to minimize release of additional evidence or rumor of wrongdoing, or attempt to defame or silence their accusers.

A large audience of potentially interested bystanders witnesses this process of accusation and defense. Other accusers, other corporations, and government enforcement agencies sometimes track efforts at labeling. Consumer complaints of unsafe products, for example, are understandably of concern to other people who use these products, other corporations that make the same or similar items, and government agencies that are supposed to protect consumers.

The audiences are important because they can sanction accused deviants whose defenses have failed. The accused corporation can be hurt if consumers boycott its products; if other corporations take the opportunity to gain some of its share of the market; or if governmental agencies regulate production, force expensive repairs, or ban the sale of its product.

Corporate deviance thus is the result of public interactions between accusing individuals, denying corporations, and an interested audience. Whether a perceived corporate harm comes to be widely labeled and responded to as deviant ultimately depends on the power of accusers as compared to that of corporations.

Illustrating the Corporate Deviance-Defining Process

Years after the Ford Pinto was first sold with fuel tank safety problems, its deficiencies became publicly apparent.[6] The fuel tank had a tendency to rupture when the car was hit from behind, even when the impact was at low speed, and sometimes the tank ignited. It is estimated conservatively that 500 burn deaths occurred between the release of the Pinto in 1970 and its recall for repairs in 1978.

A number of factors combined to bring these previously hidden problems to public attention. People injured in Pinto accidents and relatives of those killed began bringing suit against Ford. These suits slowly wound their ways through the courts, with occasionally dramatic results adding greatly to the publicity. In February of 1978, a jury awarded $128 million to a sixteen-year-old burned over 95 percent of his body.

Additionally, a biting exposé charged that the Pinto's dangers were known by some Ford officials and indirectly caused by others. Consumer advocates began to call the Pinto's problems to the attention of the media and governmental agencies. Newspaper articles and editorials increased dramatically. And the National Highway Traffic Safety Administration (NHTSA) held a series of hearings and conducted crash tests.

Ford did not remain idle in the face of efforts to call its perceived harms to the attention of outsiders. Ford officials denied that the Pinto was unsafe, inundated government officials with alternative data and interpretations, and testified at NHTSA hearings.

However, Ford's defenses were not entirely successful. In June of 1978, it was ordered to repair 1.9 million Pintos produced between 1970 and 1976. In September of the same year, it was indicted for homicide in Elkhart, Indiana, thus becoming the first corporation ever to be so charged. Ford was found not guilty after a jury trial lasting several months, but the broad publicity that the trial generated undoubtedly was not desired.

In sum, individuals and groups accused Ford of departing from important social norms by releasing an unsafe product. They alerted others to their perception and argued that something needed to be done. Ford used its considerable power to deny those accusations and was partially successful. A governmental agency ordered it to recall its products, and a jury chose not to label it criminal.

COMPLEXITIES OF THE CORPORATE DEVIANCE-DEFINING PROCESS

The Pinto episode, as well as others,[7] suggests that relationships between accusing individuals, denying corporations, and possibly responsive audiences are extremely complex. Participants frequently invoke norms that contradict one another. Additionally, potential accusers often fail to discover norm-violating behaviors of corporations. Finally, corporations have greater resources for their defense than do individual deviants. We now will examine these complexities, starting with contradictory normative environments.

The Contradictory Normative Environments of Corporations

Corporations exist in an environment where some norms contradict others. Each segment of a corporations's environment may present a reasonably coherent normative pattern, one that encourages certain actions and discourages others. But the various normative segments sometimes advance norms that conflict with one another. What one outside normative agent encourages may be discouraged by another.

For example, some outsiders argue that the corporation has a social obligation to see that the society, not just the corporation, benefits from corporate actions. Advocates of this set of norms believe that corporate objectives cannot be "limited to profit maximization alone."[8] They see single-minded pursuit of profit as departing from important corporate obligations.

There are others who argue that the only social obligation of a corporation is to maximize profits by whatever legal means are available. They consider any goal other than maximizing profit to be an attempt to influence society inappropriately and a usurpation of the rights of stockholders. Economist Milton Friedman, a leading advocate of this set of norms, has argued:

> The view has been gaining widespread acceptance that corporate officials ... have a "social responsibility" that goes beyond serving the interests of their stockholders. ... Few trends could so thoroughly undermine the very foundation of our free society as the acceptance of a social responsibility other than to make as much money for their stockholders as possible.[9]

Both of these expectations, to serve society and to maximize profits, are part of the normative environment of contemporary corporations. Some of the parties in any case in which deviance is being alleged will subscribe to each set of expectations. However, when some outsiders try to hold the corporation accountable to one set of norms, the interests of those protected by the other set generally suffer. Consider the following example.

In 1978 a stockholder of IBM asked other stockholders to support the following ban on charitable contributions: "No corporate funds ... shall be given to any charitable, educational or other similar organization, except for purposes in direct furtherance of the business interests of this corporation ... "[10] The protesting stockholder went on to explain that "over the years your company has given away millions of dollars of your money to charitable and educational institutions, money which belongs to you. Last year the total amount was $23,600,000."[11]

In response, corporate management contended that it had a legal right to contribute "reasonable sums" for charities that the board of directors judged to be "beneficial to the business activities of the corporation or the well-being of its employees."[12] Management further explained that IBM contributions equaled only one-half of 1 percent of pretax profit and that these contributions ensured the maintenance of "IBM's corporate citizenship."

At issue was a decision about who would get the $23.6 million. If held to profit maximization norms, the corporation would pay it to stockholders, with the interests of charitable and educational institutions suffering. If held to norms emphasizing corporate social responsibility, the money would be given to charity, with stockholder interests suffering.

This problem is more general then this illustration implies. Frequently, normative benefits cannot be protected for one group without a loss being suffered by another. Price-fixing may enrich stockholders and even employees, but it represents a violation of the normatively defined rights of customers. Corporate dumping of dangerous chemical wastes may harm people living near a factory, but safer disposal practices increase costs for consumers and decrease profits for stockholders.

The Hidden Nature of Corporate Deviance

For an act to be defined as deviant, an individual or group must first know that the act occurred. This sometimes is difficult because cause-effect relationships between corporate acts and their consequences are hidden.

Most cancers, for example, have long latency periods. Employees exposed to carcinogens in their work environments are not likely to contract cancer for twenty or more years.[13] When they do become ill, employees generally are not in the work settings that made them ill. Either they are not working at all or they are not working at the job they held twenty years earlier. By the time they die, they generally will have been disabled and retired and, therefore, not in any work setting. These patterns of mobility and retirement make it difficult to assign responsibility to particular exposures in most cases. Only when an illness is dramatic or unusual, involving many people or a rare form of cancer, is it likely to become known.

A related problem existed in the context of the Pinto fuel tank. A series of decisions had been made at Ford in private corporate settings where potential accusers and audiences were excluded. These decisions did not draw attention to the Pinto's dangers. Rather, Ford was indicted in response to a dramatic accident in which three young people died when their Pinto was hit from behind. The immediate cause was a van driven by a young man who admitted to Ford's defense attorneys that he used marijuana and drank beer on occasion. Prosecuting attorneys tried unsuccessfully to direct the jury's attention to more distant corporate causes of the accident.

The Ability of Corporations to Defend Themselves

Even when corporate acts become known, corporations have enormous resources with which to turn away efforts at labeling. They use their resources to build reservoirs of goodwill, provide alternative interpretations of particular problems, and attack their accusers.

Corporate attempts to build goodwill begin long before specific accusations have been made. As sociologist Edwin Sutherland observed in 1949, "The corporation attempts not only to 'fix' particular accusations against it, but also to develop good will before accusations are made."[14]

For example, Mobil Oil has been second only to Exxon in generosity to the Public Broadcasting Service.[15] These contributions are an integral part of Mobil's public relations efforts. An executive responsible for public relations felt that being

"associated with excellence" helps present the company view. A reader sees a Mobil message, and associates it with Big Oil. So he may be wary. But he also associates it with the company that brings him "Upstairs, Downstairs," so maybe he's a little more open-minded and a little more receptive.[16]

A middle-level executive said that the purpose of advertising Masterpiece Theatre is "to win credibility and . . . to provide access to, and rapport with, key groups and special publics—legislators and regulators; the press; intellectuals and academics."[17] The next level executive said, "These programs, we think, build enough acceptance to allow us to get tough on substantive issues."[18]

Having built their credibility, corporations then can provide alternative interpretations of particular social problems. In the winter of 1980, Mobil sponsored the "Edward and Mrs. Simpson" television series. Each installment was prefaced by a "fable." Each fable was lavishly produced, and each had the same message. The corporation was not responsible for the current oil crisis. Rather, the crisis was the fault of clumsy intervention and regulation of big government.

Attacking Accusers

Corporate actions are not limited to building goodwill and providing alternative interpretations. When accusations of misconduct are advanced, corporations can attempt to defend themselves by attacking their accusers. Sometimes they use socially accepted tactics by challenging the knowledge, credentials, or motives of their accusers. On occasions, as in the case of Ralph Nader,[19] they use less acceptable tactics.

Ralph Nader was born in Connecticut in 1934 and went to college at Princeton and law school at Harvard. While at Harvard, he developed an interest in auto safety. A major turning point in his career occurred in 1964, when Daniel Patrick Moynihan, then assistant secretary of labor, hired him as a consultant. Mr. Moynihan also was interested in auto safety and assigned him the task of preparing a report on that topic.

This report was evidently the original draft of Mr. Nader's first and most famous book, *Unsafe at Any Speed,*[20] a passionately angry condemnation of the auto industry. He argued that automakers deliberately ignored safety in order to increase profits. He listed accident after gruesome accident to emphasize his point. The presentation was readable, vigorous, and inflammatory. He accused automakers of homicide.

Automakers were not pleased with Mr. Nader's anger and accusations. The legal department of General Motors[21] hired a private detective agency to gather personal information about him. The legal department presumably hoped this information could be used to discredit or silence Mr. Nader, thus reducing, if not eliminating, the impact of his accusations.

However, the investigation was clumsy and came to the attention of Congress. During a committee hearing devoted to the investigation, Senator Abraham Ribicoff (Democrat, Connecticut) reviewed its scope and consequences:

> Now, let's see what happened in this case. I have the detective reports that were sent apparently to your general counsel. The detective who was following Mr. Nader reported very frequently. This is a very thick book with daily reports. It runs to many pages. . . .
> I know Winsted, Connecticut. It is a small town, in the northwest section of my state. Detectives invade this small town. They go to the high school principal and start making personal inquiries about a young man of the

town who went to high school. They ask questions of private citizens. They go to his boyhood friends and start asking pertinent questions. They go to a small town like Winsted and ask questions whether a man like Ralph Nader was anti-Semitic. They ask questions about his sex habits. They go into questions about his employment, who his friends were, why isn't a man like this at his age married? What grades did he get? Would you hire him? Now it doesn't take very long for people to start repeating that. Before you know it, you have a man who was led a private and honorable life having reflections cast upon his entire character, and that of his family, because of these questions that detectives, who basically aren't sensitive, ask about a man by the name of Ralph Nader . . . Now . . . on January 17 . . . the committee. . . . [announced] it would resume its hearings on the Federal role in traffic safety and that Ralph Nader would be one of the witnesses. . . . At that point the detective agency employed by General Motors placed Mr. Nader under constant surveillance. No longer was it just a question of asking questions in his home town and at the university that he went to and among his friends and associates in Hartford, Connecticut, where he had been associated in the practice of law. But now he was placed under surveillance. He was being followed. When he went into a restaurant to eat, detectives saw who he was eating with and what he ordered for lunch. They got the names of the taxicabs he was riding in. They followed him when he went into a bank to make a deposit or make a withdrawal. They tried to determine what hours he kept in the roominghouse where he lived.[22]

In sum, we are proposing that the corporate deviance-defining process is best understood as involving accusers, corporations, and audiences. However, corporate power, together with contradictory norms and hidden corporate acts, complicates the process. As a result, corporations only occasionally are labeled deviant. However, it still is possible to categorize the types of acts that infrequently are labeled deviant in the United States and similar societies.

TYPES OF CORPORATE DEVIANCE

Our goal now is to describe four types of corporate acts that can be labeled deviant. We will proceed by adapting a *cui bono* (who benefits) typology of formal organizations developed by sociologists Peter M. Blau and W. Richard Scott.[23]

The Blau and Scott typology focuses in part on groups that have socially defined rights to benefit from an organization's activities. It identifies four categories, each with its own needs, problems, and expected benefits. The categories are owners, employees, customers, and the public-at-large.

Business organizations have obligations to show a satisfactory profit for thier owners. They are also expected to provide employees with reasonable wages, safe working conditions, and secure retirement benefits. They are expected to provide customers with goods that are competitively priced and free of known or knowable hazards. And they are obligated to minimize release of toxic substances that injure the public-at-large.

However, stockholders have little control of corporations that once were really controlled by their owners, workers have little control of their means of supporting themselves, and customers and the public-at-large have few real choices regarding their relationships with corporations. As a result, these groups have entitlements that they may not receive, and so they may seek to label a corporation deviant.

Corporate acts thus can be labeled deviant if they fail to deliver benefits to one or more entitled groups. We now will illustrate our observations about the groups, rights, and processes involved, starting with corporate deviance against owners.

Deviance Against Owners

A typical large corporation is owned by stockholders who are uninvolved, unorganized, and collectively inarticulate.[24] They usually know very little about their corporation or the people who manage it in their names. Few of them attend the ceremonial annual meetings the corporation must hold. If they exercise their votes at boards of directors elections or on a narrow range of policies, they do so under a proxy voting mechanism loaded in favor of existing management.

Stockholder involvement is passive with little personal identity at stake and relatively little individual dependence on the corporation. Except in a few firms where families still are actively involved though not necessarily dominant (Gulf, Du Pont), stockholder control through participation in management is negligible.

As stockholding owners have lost most of the responsibilities and powers of corporate governance, so too have their rights been eroded. Stockholders now are entitled to little more than an absence of enormous problems. Management can avoid being labeled and sanctioned for deviance if it merely avoids flagrant self-dealing and if it maintains reasonably stable, although not necessarily maximum, levels of profit and economic stability. Unless stock prices or dividends decline precipitously, the norm is that stockholders should trade their stock if they are dissatisfied. They are normatively entitled to only a minimum of information for making such decisions. And they have no meaningful organized and legitimate interactions with their corporation.

Nevertheless, unusual circumstances do produce known cases where even these minimal rights are violated. They typically occur when corporations issue false information to stockholders, when insiders engage in extreme self-dealing at owners' expense, or when stockholders go to court to try to protect or expand their rights. But false information and self-dealing usually are well hidden, and stockholder legal actions attempting to protect or expand their rights, broadly defined, accounted for only about two lawsuits per major corporation over a seven-year period.[25] Thus a deviant label currently can be attached only when corporate assets are threatened and losses are great or when insider self-dealing at the expense of stockholders is blatant.

When they become known, such incidents often are quite spectacular. Consider the case of Four Seasons Nursing Centers.[26] In 1963, Oklahoma land developers and a Texas nursing home operator started a chain of nursing homes with a building design intended to improve efficiency. In 1966, Medicare went into effect and gave a great boost to their business. It also increased the demand for nursing home stock, including theirs. In 1967 they incorporated in Delaware,[27] and in 1968 they sold shares to the public. During that year the corporation raised $9 million to finance its growth.

The stockholders who bought shares knew very little. They had to rely primarily on the extraordinarily optimistic forecasts put out by Four Seasons officers and on public financial information produced by the company and its public accounting firm. Both were inaccurate. Forecasts consistently and grossly exaggerated reasonable expectations. Financial information contained such irregularities that, in an unusual action, three auditors from the accounting firm were indicted (but ultimately not found guilty) for fraud. In one situation, a part of Four Seasons would sell nursing home buildings to another part of the same company. Although no real profits could come from such a transaction, profits were recorded, and they were recorded using techniques that exaggerated income even further.

Company insiders knew that the Four Seasons shares were not what members of the public thought they were. Insiders knew of the firm's reality, whereas stockholders were ill-informed and marginally involved. The gap between stockholder and insider knowledge is shown in this excerpt from a secret memo written shortly before the firm sold its shares to the public:

Let's get our [investment banker's] opinion as to when we could sell a sizable portion of our stock, while the stock is at a good price, to guard against having to sell after the public realized that nursing homes will not meet expectations on earnings.[28]

In 1968 stockholders were buying shares for $11. In 1969 the same equity in the company cost as much as $180. In mid-1970 Four Seasons went into bankruptcy, and stockholders lost an estimated $200 million. A few fines were imposed, and two insiders received one-year prison sentences.

Deviance Against Employees

Employees perhaps have the greatest corporate involvement among normative beneficiaries of American corporations. They are extremely dependent on a single corporation, so they have the highest potential for economic benefit or harm. So too with their health and life-quality.

Employees also have the greatest subjective sense of involvement. They view themselves, and others view them, in light of their employer.[29] Compared to other beneficiaries, they realize that they are in some ways personally affected by what happens to their employer. The corporation and the union provide symbolic expressions of employees as a collectivity, and employees are treated by others as a collectivity. Compared to most other groups, they have relatively homogeneous life-styles, norms, and values and have high rates of interaction.

Employees can sometimes assert their rights strongly. Political processes since the rise of large corporations in America have produced considerable protection. Safety laws, for instance, have reinforced, sometimes in one industry at a time, the belief that employees deserve a work environment as free of hazards as reasonably can be expected. Provisions change, and expected precautions in coal mines still are different from those in offices, but some level of protection is expected and periodically enforced. By tradition and recently by law,[30] profit cannot be made by recklessly expending human life.

Kawecki Berylco[31] is a leading manufacturer of products from beryllium, a relatively rare metallic compound found in nature only in combination with other minerals. It is used in producing an expanding number of products ranging from fluorescent lamps to aircraft to sheet metal for nuclear physics research.

Beryllium manufacturing is dangerous. Its dust and fumes are toxic even after brief exposures, causing coughing, chest pain, shortness of breath, weakness, weight loss, and skin lesions.[32] Beryllium disease is slowly progressive and has a 30 pecent mortality rate.

The toxic effects of exposure to beryllium dust and fumes have long been recognized. Prior to 1942, Russian, German, and Italian medical journals contained reports of beryllium disease. Reports of beryllium poisoning and death appeared in American medical journals, starting in 1943, with many focusing on beryllium diseases among fluorescent lampworkers. And in 1952 the physician Harriet Hardy started a beryllium disease registry in Massachusetts. By the mid-1950s earlier reports, when combined with Dr. Hardy's data, made it clear that beryllium dust and fumes disabled and killed.

Kawecki Berylco Industries came to Hazelton, Pennsylvania, in 1956. Hazelton once had been the center of Pennsylvania's deep coal mining operations, but by 1955 the mines had been closed. All that remained were scattered strip-mining operations and severe unemployment. Hazelton was a town eager for industry, and Kawecki Berylco was understandably welcome. Beryllium manufacturing began in 1956, and almost immediately there were reports of illnesses among employees. Workers complained of chest pains, dry coughs, and shortness of breath. Union, state, and federal inspections revealed "excessive beryllium concentration in work place areas."[33]

Kawecki Berylco, local attorneys and physicians, and employees resisted attempts to reduce beryllium dust levels. Kawecki Berylco was bringing jobs and much needed revenue to Hazelton with net sales $61.4 million in 1970. Additionally, the federal government did not appear to take the perceived problem seriously. Total federal fines for safety violations in 1970 were only $928.

Deviance Against Customers

Customers, suppliers, and other publics-in-contact are less involved than workers with particular corporations. Customers typically purchase many products. They understandably do not spend a great deal of time collecting information prior to any particular purchase. Consequently, customers are vulnerable to a variety of injuries. Most customers, for instance, are unable to assess independently the safety of the products they buy. They do not know of the private decisions or technical problems that preceded their purchases.

The consumer movement and recent consumer protection legislation are directed at defining and protecting rights in the face of this lack of knowledge. They have only been partially successful. However, the case of the Corvair is an instance that drew great attention to the problem, and to the accuser, Ralph Nader. It produced long-run changes in auto safety, and gave consumerism a significant boost.

In the spring of 1957, General Motors decided to build the Corvair,[34] a new car that was to have a soft ride, be stylish and fuel efficient, and seat six. In order to be both small and capable of seating six, the engine would be rear-mounted to eliminate the space-robbing floor hump in most cars. In order to have a soft ride, it was weakly suspended.

Automobiles with rear-mounted engines are relatively rare because they pose special engineering problems. Foremost among these is "oversteer,"[35] caused by most of the vechicle's weight being located over the rear wheels. Two-thirds of the Corvair's weight was over its rear wheels, so even low speed and gradual turns tended to cause the car's rear to swing outward, producing a sharper turn than intended.

Weakly suspended automobiles with rear-mounted engines put enormous pressure and strain on tires when the vehicle is turning. The rear tires angle outward away from the body and toward the pavement, a problem that exaggerates the oversteer tendency. If the speed is moderate and the turn less than gentle, the metal wheel rim strikes the pavement, separating the rubber of the tire from the metal of the rim and causing an "air-out," a suddenly disastrous deflation of the tire. The result is a rollover. Here now is the complete Corvair accident: a turn causing oversteer followed by an air-out and then a rollover.

General Motors' engineers and safety personnel knew of the Corvair's problems before it was released for sale in 1959.[36] Laboratory and proving ground tests anticipated and confirmed Corvair's disastrous oversteer and air-out problems. But General Motors released the Corvair and sold 1.2 million units in five model years, with some of them causing injuries and fatalities. In 1964 and 1965, General Motors eliminated these problems by improving the Corvair's suspension system.

Deviance Against the Public-at-Large

Involvement in corporate affairs by the public-at-large occurs less often than in the case of other types of normative beneficiary. Under normal circumstances, members of the public-at-large are not economically or personally dependent on any single corporation, and they have the least personal sense of identity or common interests with a corporation.

Relationships between the public-at-large and corporations tend to be ambiguous, with few institutionalized means for regular interchange and negotiation. Additionally, the public-at-large usually is not entitled to even the equivalent of the small amounts of systematic data that stockholders receive. The public-at-large merely is entitled to go about its normal business without being interfered with or harmed by corporate action. As the case of the Love Canal[37] illustrates, however, even these minimal standards can be blatantly violated.

In the 1890s, the Love Canal near Niagara Falls, New York, was dug to provide water, power, and recreation for a new town. The town was never built because its developers went bankrupt. Its promise lost, Love Canal became none of the things its name seems to imply.

The Hooker Chemical and Plastics Corporation purchased the Love Canal site in 1947 and used it as a dump for toxic chemical wastes. It dumped thousands of metal drums containing eighty-two different toxic and carcinogenic chemical waste compounds into the waters of the canal or buried them in its banks. By 1952 the Love Canal had been filled with 21,800 tons of toxic chemicals, and Hooker donated the canal and the land surrounding it to the local school board for one dollar. The school board used part of the former dump site to build a school and sold the rest to a developer, who built 200 raised ranch homes in the early 1970s. By 1976 nearly 1,000 families lived in the Love Canal area.

In June of 1958, Jerome Wilkenfield, industrial waste supervisor for Hooker, received a call from the Niagara Falls Pollution Control Department indicating that children playing at the former dump site had received chemical burns. Mr. Wilkenfield sent several subordinates to inspect. They reported that drums had ruptured, exposing children not only to chemical burns but also to toxic fumes. Hooker executives discussed this report and its alarming implications. They decided not to inform the school board of hazards at the site because they feared legal action might force an expensive clean-up operation.

Some twenty years later Hooker personnel made a second inspection, one probably occasioned by reports of serious health problems among Love Canal residents. This inspection revealed that the area was "contaminated with organics" and these materials were "traveling laterally throughout the landfill."[38] Monitoring of the air revealed levels 250 to 5,000 times higher than those considered safe. As before, Hooker did nothing.

In August of 1978, New York State Health Commissioner Dr. Robert P. Whalen took action. He declared that the members of the general public living in the Love Canal area were in "great and immediate peril."[39] Pregnant women and children under two were evacuated, and the school closed. The president declared a federal disaster, and the state began purchasing 239 homes. In November 1979, a federal report indicated that Love Canal residents had odds as high as one in ten to contract cancer. In May of 1980, federal officials reported tentative indications that residents had high rates of chromosome damage. Angry residents responded by holding two environmental officials hostage for five hours, and the federal government then agreed to move the residents of an additional 700 homes.

Hooker has stonewalled the Love Canal problem and maintained a low and protective profile throughout. Its 1953 deed contained a disclaimer of responsbility for any injuries that might occur because of the buried chemicals. It has denied that the chemicals directly caused illnesses or chromosome damage. But it is being sued by the Justice Department for $125 million for four different chemical dumps in Niagara Falls and by New York State for $635 million for its responsibility specifically at Love Canal.

SUMMARY

In these first two chapters we have provided a corporate deviance framework. We first showed that corporations are real and that corporate positions and coalitions produce corporate actions. Then we examined the corporate deviance-defining process, suggesting that it includes accusers, corporations, and audiences. Finally, we showed that the defining process can result in a corporation's being labeled deviant for violating the normative rights of owners, employees, customers, or the public-at-large.

We now will apply this framework to each of the four types of deviance, beginning with deviance against owners.

ANNOTATED SELECTED READINGS

Conklin, John E. *Illegal but Not Criminal: Business Crime in America.* Englewood Cliffs, NJ: Prentice-Hall, 1977. Synthesis and analysis of available evidence on the nature and causes of crimes by executives and corporations.

Ermann, M. David, and Richard J. Lundman, eds. *Corporate and Governmental Deviance: Problems of Organizational Behavior in Contemporary Society.* New York: Oxford U. P., 1978. Collection of works about deviance and criminality by corporations and governments.

Geis, Gilbert, and Robert M. Meier, eds. *White-Collar Crime: Offenses in Business, Politics, and the Professions.* New York: The Free Press, 1977. Collection of classic analyses on white-collar crime as well as more recent materials. Includes especially thoughtful introductory essays.

Johnson, John M. and Jack D. Douglas, eds. *Crime At The Top: Deviance in Business and the Professions.* Philadelphia: Lippincott, 1978. Collection descriptive of deviance and criminality by business people and professionals.

Sutherland, Edwin N. *White-Collar Crime.* New York: Holt, Rinehart and Winston, 1949. Classic study describing crime by seventy large corporations and interpreting them in terms of differential association theory.

NOTES

1. Earl Rubington and Martin S. Weinberg, eds., *Deviance: The Interactionist Perspective*, 2d ed. (New York: Macmillan, 1973), p. vii.
2. Marshall E. Blume and Irwin Friend, "The American Stockholder," *The Wharton Magazine* (Srping 1978): 32.
3. "The 500 Largest Industrial Corporations," *Fortune* (May 5, 1980): 275.
4. Ibid., p. 275.
5. James S. Coleman, *Power and the Structure of Society* (New York: Norton, 1974), pp. 104–106. See also Albert O. Hirschman, *Exit, Voice and Loyalty* (Cambridge, MA: Harvard U. P., 1970).
6. Materials for this section are primarily from Ronald C. Kramer, "The Ford Pinto Homicide Prosecution: Criminological Questions and Issues Concerning the Control of Corporate Crime" (paper presented at the annual meeting of the American Society of Criminology, Philadelphia, November 9, 1979), and Victoria Lynn Swigert and Ronald A. Farrell, "Definitional Processes Leading to the Homicide Indictment Against the Ford Motor Company" (paper presented at the annual meeting of the Society for the Study of Social Problems, Boston, August 1979).
7. For example, see Neal Shover, "The Criminalization of Corporate Behavior: Federal Surface Coal Mining," in Gilbert Geis and Ezra Stotland, eds., *White-Collar Crime* (Beverly Hills, CA: Sage Publications, 1980), pp. 98–125.
8. Richard Eels, "A Philosophy for Corporate Giving," *The Conference Record* 5 (January 1968): 16.
9. Milton Friedman, *Capitalism and Freedom* (Chicago: University of Chicago Press, 1962), pp. 133–134.
10. International Business Machines, *Notice of 1978 Annual Meeting and Proxy Statement.* (New York: IBM Stockholder Relations Department), p. 17.
11. International Business Machines, *Notice*, p. 17.
12. International Business Machines, *Notice*, p. 18.
13. William J. Blot et al., "Lung Cancer After Employment in Shipyards During World War II," *The New England Journal of Medicine* 299 (September 21, 1978): 623.
14. Edwin H. Sutherland, *White-Collar Crime* (New York: Holt, Rinehart and Winston, 1949), p. 32.
15. The following argument is adapted from M. David Ermann, "The Operative Goals of Corporate Philanthropy: Contributions to the Public Broadcasting Service, 1972–1976," *Social Problems* 25 (June 1978): 504–514.
16. Quoted in Irwin Ross, "Public Relations Isn't Kid-Glove Stuff at Mobil," *Fortune* 94 (September 1976): 110.
17. Quoted in Philis S. McGarath, ed., *Business Credibility: The Critical Factors* (New York: The Conference Board, 1976), p. 30.

18. Quoted in Ross, "Public Relations," p. 110.
19. The material on Ralph Nader is based upon Robert Buckhorn, *Nader: The People's Lawyer* (Englewood Cliffs, NJ: Prentice-Hall, 1972), and Charles McCarry, *Citizen Nader* (New York: Saturday Review Press, 1975).
20. Ralph Nader, *Unsafe at Any Speed: The Designed-in Dangers of the American Automobile* (New York: Grossman, 1965).
21. The material descriptive of General Motors' action is based upon U.S. Senate, 98th Congress, 2nd Session, March 23, 1966, "Hearings Before the Subcommittee on Executive Reorganizations of the Committee on Government Operations," *Traffic Safety*, Part 4, pp. 1381–1399, and S. Prakash Sethi, *Up Against the Corporate Wall* (Englewood Cliffs, NJ: Prentice-Hall, 1971), pp. 189–214.
22. U.S. Senate, "Hearings," pp. 1396–1397.
23. This section is adapted from Peter M. Blau and W. Richard Scott, *Formal Organizations* (San Francisco: Chandler, 1962), pp. 42–54.
24. Coleman, *Power*, pp. 38–44.
25. Thomas M. Jones, "Stockholders and the Corporation: A New Relationship," *Journal of Contemporary Business* 8 (1979): 93–94.
26. Materials on the Four Seasons case are from Frederick D. Sturdivant and Larry M. Robinson, *The Corporate Social Challenge: Cases and Commentaries* (Homewood, IL: Richard D. Irwin, 1977), pp. 3–16, and Lester A. Sobel, *Corruption in Business* (New York: Facts on File, 1977), pp. 169–170.
27. Delaware incorporation is popular with insiders partly because Delaware laws give little protection to stockholders. See Chapter 7 of this book. Also see Ted Nicholas, *How to Form Your Own Corporation Without a Lawyer for Under $50.00* (Wilmington, Delaware Enterprise Publishing Company, 1972), p. 6.
28. Quoted in Sturdivant and Robinson, *Corporate*, p. 11.
29. Asked, "What work does your parent do?" many people omit personal traits or occupations and simply name an employer.
30. The Occupational Safety and Health Act of 1970 (Public Law 91–596) requires an employer to "furnish to each of his employees employment and a place of employment which are free from recognized hazards that are causing or are likely to cause death or serious physical harm to his employees."
31. Material on Kawecki Berylco Industries is based upon Rachel Scott, *Muscle and Blood* (New York: E. P. Dutton, 1974), pp. 35–54; Jeffrey Reiman, *The Rich Get Richer and the Poor Get Prison* (New York: Wiley, 1979), p. 71; and Harriet Hardy, "Beryllium Poisoning—Lessons in Control of Man-Made Disease," *The New England Journal of Medicine* 273 (November 25, 1965): 1188–1199.
32. Morton M. Ziskind, "Occupational Pulmonary Disease," *Clinical Symposia* 30 (1978): 19.
33. Reiman, *The Rich Get Richer*, p. 71.
34. Discussion of the Corvair is based upon Nader, *Unsafe*.

35. Ibid., p. 21.
36. Ibid., pp. 21–36.
37. This section is based upon newspaper articles appearing in the following papers on the dates indicated: *The New York Times,* Section A, 2 August 1978, pp. 1,9; Section A, 3 August 1978, pp.1, 8; Section B, 4 August 1978, p. 14; Section A, 5 August 1978, pp. 1, 20, 18; Section A, 6 August 1978, p. 24; Section B, 9 August 1978, p. 1; Section B, 11 April 1979, pp. 1,4; Section A, 20 May 1980, p. 1; Section B, 20 May 1980, p. 4; Section A, 21 May 1980, p. 1; Section B, 21 May 1980, p. 6; *The Washington Post,* Section A, 11 April 1979, pp.1, 12; *The Columbus Dispatch,* Section A, 11 April 1979, p. 11.
38. *The Washington Post,* Section A, 11 April 1979, p. 1.
39. *The New York Times,* Section A, 3 August 1978, p. 1.

TWO

Types of corporate deviance

3

Deviance against owners

[Even] late 19th century courts ... recognized that corporations do not necessarily maximize the wealth of the shareholders because, in a variety of ways, corporate managers might be maximizing their own wealth. In response to this risk of self-enrichment, corporate legal doctrine provides a general imperative to persons controlling corporations: thou shalt not unfairly use what beneficially belongs to others.
—*David M. Phillips* [1]

37

Large American corporations today have stockholders who officially own them and managers who attempt to run them. The law for some time has recognized that under such circumstances corporate insiders such as managers, board members, and major shareholders can readily use their positions to violate stockholders' rights. In fact, since the late nineteenth century, legal protections have evolved to deal with corporate insiders who violate stockholders' opportunities to benefit from the fact that they are owners.[2]

As the law currently stands, insiders are required to be "fair" in their running of a corporation in order to protect shareholders who lack control. Insiders may not usurp investment opportunities available to the corporation. They may not manipulate assets to perpetuate their own control. Their personal dealings with the corporation must not harm the corporation. "Corporate insiders are not permitted to make unfair use of corporate assets . . ."[3]

Furthermore, managers may not take compensation so excessive that it actually amounts to wasting the corporation's assets. In the most celebrated case dealing with this issue, the Supreme Court ruled that compensation cannot be "so large as in substance and effect to amount to spoilation of corporate property."[4] Insiders also may not profit by buying and selling shares on the basis of knowledge they have gained through their inside positions, and they are required to take due care in exercising reasonable skills and diligence in carrying out their duties.

Of course, there often are vagueness, discretion, change, and inequity in the implementation of these stockholder protections. But there is also broad agreement on the values underlying ownership rights, and a significant amount of stockholder protection does exist. Managers thus risk public disapproval and personal sanction when they too obviously fail to meet their obligations to stockholders.

Preview of the Chapter

The purpose of this chapter is to describe and analyze corporate actions contrary to the socially defined and enforced rights of stockholders. We will discuss the dynamic and often conflict-based nature of stockholder rights, we will examine in detail one recent example of corporate deviance against stockholders, and we will address the question of why corporations sometimes act contrary to the interest of their owners.

In describing these actions, we will challenge the prevailing images of the origins of involvement by individual managers. Deviance against owners is not necessarily an innocent outgrowth of lower- and middle-level employees taking necessary shortcuts in order to meet the conflicting or impossible demands unwittingly imposed on them by top management. Very top level personnel often are involved in corporate deviance, either directly or as shapers of the culture of the organization.[5]

In analyzing corporate deviance against owners, we will show that techniques of corporate deviance flow directly from the normal operation of a business. Special procedures generally are not required because deviance easily can be accommodated as part of routine operations. As the case study for this chapter shows, even computers are used in ways essentially similar to how they are used in more conventional circumstances.

We also will analyze how long-term changes in owner-corporate relations make deviance against stockholders possible. The declining involvement of owners, as management and stockholding become separate, makes owners more vulnerable. This is compounded by the growing size of corporations, which makes control by anyone at all more difficult. However, we will suggest that as stockholdings become reconcentrated in pension funds and other institutional investors, the power of owners may again be enhanced; and deviance against them, reduced.

SOCIAL CHANGE AND NORMATIVE OWNERSHIP RIGHTS

Owners' rights to hold, use, and sell things of value are variable and impermanent. At any given time some societies permit—and others constrain—ownership rights to land, factories, or slaves. Rights of ownership for property and people changed with the coming of land reform to Latin American land owners, socialism to Russian factory owners, and emancipation to American slave owners. Socially defined ownership rights thus are changeable rather than fixed. In fact, ownership rights to productive property can change dramatically within individual societies, and they do differ greatly between societies. Nowhere is this illustrated better than by comparing postrevolutionary changes of ownership rights in the Soviet Union[6] to those in the United States. Soviet ownership rights have changed often and differ greatly from their American equivalents. However, ownership rights in the United States also have been variable.

Ownership Rights in the Soviet Union

With the Russian Revolution of 1917 came a disassembling of the previous czarist laws. Among the laws changed were those about ownership rights to productive property. Persons who owned land, multiple dwellings, basic industries, and other means of production lost their ownership. However, some rights of ownership to such productive property were reintroduced five years after the revolution in order to attract foreign investment to replace that which had been destroyed by wars. In 1928 changes were made, and once more private ownership of productive capacity was dramatically reduced, this time because attracting foreign capital had become a less important concern.

Through all these changes, the political realities of productive property were intimately intertwined with laws regarding their ownership. Defining who had what ownership rights to what assets was correctly seen as influencing other societal realities. According to Marxist theory, private ownership of the means of production is the basic division in society. Abolition of rights to this type of private ownership is thus the major purpose of a socialist revolution:

> While the faithful producer has been rewarded in a manner which sometimes appears munificent, he has never been permitted to have that type of property which in the eyes of Soviet theorists would permit him to challenge the power of the regime.... The faithful will be rewarded by many things, wealth, position, medals, and privileges, but they will not be accorded an opportunity to become a new generation of landlords and industrialists.[7]

Ownership Rights in the United States

In the United States, rights to productive property differ radically from those in the Soviet Union, presumably because of differing social and economic forces. Individual ownership of productive property is encouraged, with great self-congratulation because corporations are not owned by the government. American conventional belief holds that governmental ownership produces inefficiency, whereas nongovernmental ownership produces efficiency or at least is virtuous. Texaco, for instance, has run a series of television advertisements showing the ordinary Americans who own its stock. A.T.&T. is proud that over three million persons and institutions own its stock, more than is true of any other corporation. This encouragement of private ownership of productive resources, it often is argued, is a conservative force in American society and is encouraged for that reason.

American rights in this area have not been stagnant either. Unlike the situation in the Soviet Union, however, ownership rights have expanded rather than contracted. In the early years of American corporations, management responsibilities and owners' profit rights were quite different from what they are today. Each corporation first was expected to serve the public good. State legislatures would not issue charters unless the public service was clear. Indeed, "It was not until the middle of the nineteenth century that a profit-making commitment to stockholders was formulated as the major corporate goal. In the process, what was once management's obligation to contribute to the public good became a matter of personal taste [of managers]."[8] Parallel to the declining emphasis on serving the public was a growing emphasis on serving stockholders.

Undoubtedly, American norms for corporate goals will continue to change in the future. For example, rights of owners could change radically if there were radical changes in our current political and legal arrangements:

> When an employee is convicted of embezzlement and ordered to make restitution, it affirms the legitimacy of the employer's priority over the employee in determining how the funds shall be used. [However,] if the government that makes that decree is overthrown in a revolution, the employee may be able to use the power of the new government to make the employer surrender the funds to him.[9]

In sum, ownership rights in the Soviet Union, the United States, or elsewhere are changeable and dynamically intertwined with the changing social conditions of a society. The balance of this chapter focuses on norms as they exist and change in contemporary American society.

DEVIANCE AGAINST AMERICAN STOCKHOLDERS

Episodes of deviance by corporate insiders against stockholders appear to have been frequent in the early 1900s. According to one estimate, during the decade before the stock market crash of 1929, "fully half of some $50 billion worth of new securities floated in the United States became worthless."[10] Various states responded to these abuses by passing Blue Sky laws against "speculative schemes which have no more basis than so many feet of blue sky."[11] States, however, were limited in what they could accomplish because their actions were limited to intrastate sales of securities. Owners or potential owners could still be victimized by corporations located outside a particular state.

It was in this context that Franklin Roosevelt, in the famous first one hundred days of his administration, requested and received legislation to regulate security sales. A year later additional legislation was passed, and an enforcement agency, the Securities and Exchange Commission (SEC), was founded. Although the SEC's founding was precipitated partially by the stock market crash, more fundamentally it represented a response to unsavory practices that long had existed in securities sales. These practices had flourished because investors could be deprived of sufficient or sufficiently accurate information for judging securities.

The SEC, therefore, tries to protect security purchasers by increasing the amount and quality of information available to them. In fact, the law often was called the "Truth in Securities" Act. It requires that most security offerings be registered with the SEC and that registration be accompanied by a range of accurate and useful information, including earnings, assets, and leadership. The SEC requires all public sellers of securities to make this information available to potential buyers.

The prevailing consensus is that the SEC has enhanced rights of stock buyers as against those of sellers.[12] But it also has had its failures. The most glaring recent failure is the Equity Funding scandal, one of the largest frauds uncovered in recent American history and in many ways suggestive of explanations of this type of deviance.

The Equity Funding Scandal[13]

Equity Funding began with an innovative idea in the late 1950s. Equity would sell mutual fund shares to customers who then would borrow against their shares in order to pay for life insurance policies. Customers could simultaneously have life insurance protection and put aside a nest egg invested in the mutual fund. Equity Funding would sell the mutual funds and insurance as a package.

The seeds of the fraud date to 1964, when the still small company led by two aggressive young innovators decided to sell its idea and its corporate shares on the public market. Its financial statement of that year contained a nonexistent asset of more than $6 million, exaggerating the financial assets and success of the initially successful firm in order to attract potential stockholders. As described in a subsequent investigation, the conspiracy appeared "to have been initially motivated . . . by an obsessive desire on the part of its participants to inflate and keep aloft the market price of the common stock."[14] Their motives apparently were to drive up Equity shares to the point where they could be used to buy up legitimate companies. The amount of overstated assets and sales continued to rise rapidly:

What was finally happening was simply that Equity Funding was purchasing phony life insurance for nonexistent mutual fund-holders with phony loans. Phony insurance sales generated phony profits. And the phony profits kept Equity stock flying high.[15]

Phony customers were large in number. When the fraud was discovered, there were 56,000 bogus policies as compared to only 41,000 real ones. There also were accounting irregularities that claimed $200 million in nonexistent assets.

Most of the time, bogus policies were fabricated using computers to create fictitious customers automatically. A simple entry on the computer tape of a fictitious name, address, age, and policy amount was sufficient to continue the fraud. The conspirators' real work came when the Equity's outside auditing firm, in accordance with SEC requirements, asked for a small sample of application forms, employment and medical histories, and other paperwork to verify that customers actually existed. In these cases, more elaborate measures had to be taken.

At times, the needed false records were created at a "manufacturing party," such as the one held in a corporate conference room from six until ten on an evening in early 1971. Many middle-level management people were there and wandered in and out in the course of the party. A good time was had by all, with lots of laughs from such activities as creating humorous names for fictitious examining doctors. Use of a variety of pens and rubber stamps to avoid suspicious uniformity were among the many precautions taken at these parties.

A more routine method of creating false records also existed. At an office a few miles from headquarters, a dozen young clerks prepared false records according to a manual specifically prepared for that purpose. They could create up to fifteen or twenty bogus customers on busy days, but most of their time they had nothing to do, so they partied for almost any excuse, took some drugs, and simply talked. None appeared to know what they were involved in, and none were indicted when the fraud was exposed. They were just doing the kinds of things clerks everywhere do, but in this case it was an integral part of a massive fraud.

The fraud itself was the creation of two innovative executives, one who represented Equity to Wall Street and the other responsible for management of the firm. Together they were an effective team, attracting numerous investors and creating stock market enthusiasm for their company. But these two executives could not have pulled off such a scandal themselves. They had help from a number of other persons, each of whom performed some specialized part of their conspiracy. Many did not know its entire scope, and a few probably knew little of what was happening. But together, their individual efforts added up to a massive fraud. Those indicted for the conspiracy were the following:

- The forty-six-year-old president and chairman of the board, one of the originators of the scheme. (The other had died in a freak accident in 1970.)
- The thirty-four-year-old executive vice-president and chief investment and financial officer.
- The thirty-six-year-old executive vice-president and head of insurance operations.
- The fifty-nine-year-old senior administrative vice-president, who resigned in 1969.
- The thirty-year-old comptroller.
- The thirty-five-year-old vice-president of insurance operations.
- The thirty-year-old chief actuary.
- The twenty-nine-year-old assistant to the comptroller.
- The thirty-one-year-old vice-president for insurance accounting.
- The thirty-three-year-old vice-president of the insurance subsidiary.
- The thirty-five-year-old lawyer for the insurance subsidiary.
- The thirty-two-year-old former comptroller.
- The thirty-two-year-old assistant in the comptroller's office.
- The thirty-four-year-old reinsurance department manager.
- The thirty-two-year-old ex-reinsurance department manager, who left in 1970.
- A twenty-five-year old computer programmer.
- The fifty-year-old partner in Equity's accounting firm.
- The forty-four-year-old local audit manager for the accounting firm.
- The thirty-three-year-old president of an Equity subsidiary.
- The twenty-five-year-old supervisor of the twelve clerks who helped create false records.
- The twenty-seven-year-old supervisor responsible for making sure policy details were in order.
- The twenty-eight-year-old supervisor of the company printshop.
- The thirty-six-year-old head of computer programming.
- The former life insurance comptroller (age not available).
- The thirty-seven-year-old ex-subsidiary vice-president (who exposed the fraud and was an indicted co-conspirator).[16]

In 1973 their story was exposed by the last person on the list, an ex-middle-level manager upset because he had been fired in an austerity drive. After his disclosure, the company went into bankruptcy on security that had been valued at $300 million in stock and $200 million in bonds. There had been a total of 10,000 stockholders, with half the stock owned by pension funds and other institutional investors. Some of these individual shareholders suffered severe losses:

A couple . . . said their son was a college student in desperate need of an operation. The parents had begged, borrowed and scraped together enough money to invest in the hope that the security they selected would show near-term growth to finance the medical costs. The stock they selected was Equity Funding. They purchased 500 shares just a few days before trading in the security was suspended. . . . All the family's savings went down the drain with Equity Funding, and so did their son's chances of getting the operation.[17]

Analysis of Equity Funding

The atmosphere that evolved in the company over its early years of aggressive salesmanship and spectacular growth appears to have contributed to later deviant acts. This atmosphere encouraged freewheeling excesses, some probably within the law and others clearly outside it. As one participant explained, like accountants in other aggressive business situations, he had "played games with numbers."[18] This lax atmosphere seems to have come from the very top of the company, where the documented excesses of acceptable business behavior were most clearly found. The court-appointed trustee who ran the company after bankruptcy compared the Equity fraud to Watergate:

> You cannot have a fraud of this nature without it being conducted from the top. I don't know if Nixon knew of Watergate or not. But you had to have the moral climate that reflects the top . . . people don't do things that they know isn't all right with their boss . . . otherwise they'd be scared to death they'd be caught doing them.[19]

Into this atmosphere, the leaders recruited and promoted to responsible positions a group of unusually young and inexperienced people with great ambition. The recruits were, therefore, malleable. They had little previous experience to compare to their present experience, so they had relatively unformed moral standards and commitments regarding business behavior. They knew that business dealings have rules different from everyday personal relationships, but how different was learned in practice rather than in school. Their lack of experience, combined with their personal ambition, apparently blinded Equity's young executives to the moral and legal choices they were unconsciously making. They were bright young people, "eager to progress in the corporate world, impressionable, willing, sedulous. Was this the way one made it? Then that is what one did."[20]

Deviance could be made even easier for most of the participants because each was doing only one small part of the task. Each had a specialized role, which in itself was of only limited illegality. Although the sum of these small individual acts was a massive fraud, from the perspective of each individual any particular contribution would be (or could be seen as) relatively minor:

> There were many employees at Equity Funding who performed mechanical functions on phony papers—but had no way of knowing they were phony. Others developed suspicions. Some questioned their superiors and were satisfied by explanations that seemed plausible. Others were not entirely fooled and shared their deepening mistrust of company officials with co-workers. Many became convinced there was wrongdoing but avoided confronting it directly. Some surreptitiously investigated for further confirmation of the rumors. A few spoke about specific fraudulent activities in an open fashion. [But] few knew of the staggering dimensions of the fraud; these who did were included among the men eventually indicted.[21]

The indicted supervisor of the office where the young clerks produced false records, for instance, admitted that "I didn't know the total picture of what was going on but I knew something was wrong."[22] The supervisor's ignorance of the total picture was made easy because this firm, like all large organizations, was specialized, in effect dividing employees into cells where each cell has only limited knowledge of what the others were doing. Only a few people in the inner management of Equity knew the vastness of the fraud. For the others, "Equity Funding is another instance of the blind men and the elephant."[23]

However, for these others the clear moral choice visible with the benefit of hindsight was not available when they became involved. Rarely on the first day of this involvement were they asked to choose between fully participating in the fraud or withdrawing. Rather, they were introduced to the fraud in stages, first engaging in a small shading of the truth and then increasingly larger ones. The step-at-a-time involvement was partly a matter of good psychological understanding on the part of Equity's leaders. More importantly, it reflected the way the fraud itself grew from modest beginnings. In the early stages, it was limited, and there were few dramatic decisions facing Equity employees. The more blatant frauds involving many people only grew in a "helter-skelter, hand-to-mouth" manner in the fraud's final years.

Public knowledge of the fraud probably should have come much earlier than it did. Many groups had responsibilities that ought to have alerted them that something was wrong. First were the auditors. Auditing techniques should normally detect frauds on this scale, but in Equity's case the auditors were so heavily compromised that three were criminally indicted and their firms eventually made to pay $39 million to former Equity shareholders. Second, the Board of Directors failed to exercise its important responsibility properly when it agreed to an auditing firm too small for the job, with personnel of poor reputation and ability. Finally, there were outsiders associated with the sale of various issues of Equity securities—underwriting firms, banks, the Securities and Exchange Commission, and the stock exchanges—who also should have shown more diligence and skepticism. "Equity Funding was crawling with regulators and quasi-regulators, none of whom seemed to question the staggering good fortune of a company that could virtually double sales every year, year after year."[24]

Exposure of this and most other episodes of corporate deviance is not the result of extraordinary detective work by regulatory agencies. Rather, it is the result of chance events such as accidental slipups or disgruntled employees. Even dissatisfied employees typically remained silent, usually because of their loyalty to the organization. There was, therefore, little "whistle-blowing" by people exposing their own organization's deviance.[25] Under such circumstances, detection is difficult. Equity's deviance against owners was exposed because one disgruntled ex-employee did come forth, whereas all others had remained silent. He was angered by his dismissal in an austerity drive.

Many other employees who knew parts of the scheme later said they would have reported it to regulatory authorities, but they lacked sufficient proof. For instance, Pat Hooper, vice-president of an Equity subsidiary, resigned rather than agreeing to act illegally. However, he remained long enough to install his successor, whom he warned to watch out for the illegal activities over which he was resigning. During this period, he attended a meeting and a dinner afterward with three other Equity executives:

> Hooper said almost nothing at dinner; once more, he was too dumbfounded to talk. The others were openly joking about the phony sales production figures, and, in an oblique way, it seemed to Hooper that they were joking about him. They knew he was resigning; they knew he wouldn't be able to do anything with his knowledge because he didn't have any proof.[26]

Given the ability of large corporations today to shield themselves from outsiders, even when the outsiders are owners, it appears that only frauds as massive and complex as Equity's have much vulnerability to disclosure. In less dramatic cases, the chances of exposure are even less because the extent of the fraud can be camouflaged more readily.

ANALYSIS OF DEVIANCE AGAINST OWNERS

Deviance against owners, as with the Equity Funding case, can occur only to the extent that owners lack power to enforce their normative rights. Owner power has varied over time, with control of corporations gradually shifting from owners to managers to the corporation itself. Possibilities of deviance against owners thus have increased as the locus of power has moved more distantly from them. However, power now may be returning to owners by way of different and more powerful ownership representation through large institutional investors. This final section analyzes these fundamental power changes and their implications for deviance against owners.

Owners as Power Holders[27]

It often is contended that owners have power and that deviance against them thus will be unlikely. Proponents of this view note that stockholders are well supported by the law and by corporate charters. Stockholder votes are the official sources of management's power and must be sought periodically for management to continue. Managers are legally stockholders' employees. On more routine matters, owner interests are represented by their elected representatives, the board of directors. Milton Friedman is the major advocate of this position:

> In a free-enterprise, private property system, a corporate executive is an employee of the owners of the business. He has direct responsibility to his employers. This responsibility is to conduct that business in accordance with their desires. . . .[28]

Until the 1920s, this might have been an accurate portrayal of corporate reality. It was widely held—and probably correctly in many cases—that corporations were the instruments of their owners. Andrew Carnegie controlled his steel company, and Henry Ford still had two decades before him as head of the company he had founded and that bore his name. Many corporations had one or a few owners who personally directed them. They owned their companies and made company decisions, so the company could not be deviant against them. Owners could be inept, but there existed no independent organization to be deviant against them. Theirs was the power to make corporate decisions, for they were simultaneously owners and managers.

Managers as Power Holders[29]

Ownership and control are less likely to be concurrent today. Ownership and management generally are separate, with managers having more power than owners. Of the many examples of this, none is more graphic than annual stockholder meetings. At these meetings management reigns. The proxy system of voting assures their power because of the wide dispersion of ownership and the relative noninvolvement of stockholders. Under this system, all ballots not returned by stockholders are considered to be votes for management. (It is as if all nonvoters in a presidential election were counted as voting for the incumbent.) Management thus rarely loses on issues brought to a vote of stockholders.

On issues not put to a stockholder vote, the board of directors is officially the owners' representative. But directors are much closer to management than to owners. All are nominated by management, and many work in management. The nonmanagers on a board often know very little because they are directors of many companies, and each of them gives only a small fraction of his or her time. The nonmanagers, therefore, do not effectively represent and protect stockholders.

Nor can stockholders directly represent and protect themselves. Stockholders cannot know much about what their corporation is doing, nor can they exert significant pressure on it. In fact, they typically are too distant from the everyday operation of the corporation even to suspect deviance. Such was the case with the Equity Funding scandal. Stockholders were completely unaware of it.

The observation that managers, not owners, control corporations first gained popular attention in 1932 with the landmark book by Adolph Berle and Gardiner Means, *The Modern Corporation and Private Property*.[30] They argued that ownership and control have become separated. Ownership is fragmented through the mechanism of the stock markets, with each owner having only a miniscule share of ownership and no control of the corporation. Management remains concentrated and decides what the firm is to do, with minimal restraints. The stockholder is

> left as a matter of law with little more than the loose expectation that a group of men, under a nominal duty to run the enterprise for his benefit and that of others like him, will actually observe this obligation. In almost no particular is he in a position to demand that they do or refrain from doing any given thing. Only in extreme cases will their judgment as to what is or is not in his interest be interfered with. And they have acquired under the corporate charter power to do many things which by no possibility can be considered in his interest....[31]

Deviance against owners is a likely outcome of this power imbalance because stockholder goals are not shared by managers. The stockholder's goal is a reasonably high return on investment at a reasonably low risk. But for managers, whose stock ownership interests in the firm are less important than their occupational interests, other goals can prevail. If their goals are personal profit, these will doubtless conflict with goals of owners. "In the operation of the corporation, the controlling group even if they own a large block of stock, can serve their own pockets better by profiting at the expense of the company than by making profits for it."[32] If their goals are power and prestige, they might spend some profits on high status charities or politically influential activities, although the funds might be better returned to stockholders to make their own charitable or political decisions.[33] And if professional pride motivates them, they may elevate working conditions higher than required by labor markets and unions, actions that are admirable but do not necessarily serve the long-run financial interests of stockholders. In fact, owners and managers have few objective interests in common. The position of managers allows their interests, within limits, to predominate.

This second theory of managerial power in organizations is a closer approximation of current reality and a better explainer of deviance than the earlier theory of owner power. However, it, too, contains a fundamental flaw. It assumes managers possess the ability to control their corporations. In large corporations this increasingly is not the case.

Organizations as Power Holders

The third theory holds that the tendency for power to concentrate in management hands is self-limiting.[34] At some point managers are largely captive to the size and complexity of the organization they supposedly manage. Their organization no longer is unified, acting at the command of the top leadership, except in the most dramatic cases. Rather, the corporation now is visualized best as not controlled by any person or group of persons.

With this interpretation, owners' lack of knowledge need not be interpreted as a management conspiracy to keep stockholders in the dark, although management continues to have incentives to suppress certain information. Rather, no person in management or outside can have the knowledge to control the corporation because it is so complex. Individual managers, like individual owners, have great difficulty even knowing what is going on. Management is too diffused, and decisions require the knowledge and coordination of numerous managers. These managers individually lack the resources to make important decisions. They instead are dependent on other managers for the knowledge and power needed for any action to be taken.[35] What single manager could sufficiently understand the $16.3 billion sales and 292,000 employees at IBM to control it or even have a good sense of what the corporation is doing?

The organization literally has taken on a life of its own. Power is not the power of people, for all people are replaceable. Motivation is not the motivation of people, for action is determined by the positions the people occupy within organizations. As James Coleman has observed, the organization is more powerful and more important than the people who nominally own or run it:

> In this circumstance, a condition can arise which is wholly new to society: one person can suffer a loss of power without another person receiving a corresponding gain. The sum total of power among persons in society is no longer constant, because of the new set of actors which have power in themselves—power that resides in the corporate actor and does not accrue to any person connected to that corporate actor. This is a difficult but important distinction ... The point is that the power held by corporate bodies (whether business corporations, trade unions, government bodies, or still another form) is in the hands of no person, but resides in the corporate actor itself.[36]

These new realities exist because corporate management has grown more complex since the 1920s. Unlike the early Ford Motor Company, modern corporations can no longer be run by a single person, for no person has the breadth of knowledge and skills to make the kinds of diverse and often technical decisions that have to be made. The original Henry Ford did not realize this, and as his company grew, he almost ruined it. Management is now in hands of managers who themselves are the agents of the corporation and play out roles within it. The structure of these roles is becoming the most important influence on corporate behavior.

It would appear that contemporary corporate deviance against owners is best understood as the result of a number of trends associated with the growth of organizations. When corporations were small, it was reasonable to argue that owners controlled their organizations and that deviance against them was logically impossible because the organization was their agent. Such was the case with Henry Ford's car company and Harvey Firestone's tire company. As corporations grew larger, owners surrendered their control to managers, leaving the possibility of deviance such as the Equity Funding case. Now there may be deviance against owners because corporations are so large that they cannot be controlled by either managers or owners.

Institutional Investors and the Future of Deviance Against Owners

However, power now may be returning to owners by way of different and more powerful ownership representation. Formal ownership of large corporations is undergoing still another significant change.[37] Numerous small stockholders are being replaced by "institutional investors" who are fewer in number but much larger in size. These institutional investors (banks, insurance companies, investment firms, foundations, universities) now account for 70 percent of the buying and selling of stocks on the New York Stock Exchange. By the year 2000 more than half of corporate stock probably will be controlled by institutional investors. Large corporations thus will be answerable primarily to other large organizations that will hold the majority of their voting stock.

Institutional investors may then marshal and concentrate the power of previously powerless owners into substantial blocks of stock that can influence the ongoing behaviors of corporations. With such large shares in a given company, typical institutional investors will not have the individual small investors' option of selling stock if they disapprove of what the company is doing. A large institutional investor selling its shares in a company could severely depress the price of its remaining shares during the time it is selling. Institutional investors of the future, therefore, will be captives of their own wealth and power. They likely will have to exercise their power because to switch investments would cause them to lose some of their wealth. In the course of exercising their power, they will become a substantial outside force representing stockholders, the first such force in fifty years.

Whether institutions will exercise their power for or against stockholders or whether they will exercise power at all is unclear. There is a long-established "Wall Street rule" that investors should either support a company's management or sell their shares in that company. However, the Wall Street rule is becoming less and less feasible. Exceptions are appearing, and the exceptions are becoming more numerous. Many institutional investors during the 1970s set up proxy committees to decide how to vote on the various issues put before stockholders for a vote. Typically, they vote negatively on proposals that they feel unduly enrich management at stockholder expense or dilute the relative value of a share of stock. This type of voting seems to protect directly the interest of owners in a way impossible for an individual owner.

SUMMARY

The Equity Funding scandal shows that corporate deviance against owners can occur because owners lack power to enforce their normative rights. Equity Funding elites could violate stockholder rights because of the separation of ownership from management.

However, recent evidence indicates that ownership and control patterns once again are changing. The power to control may be shifting in the direction of institutional investors.

What does all this mean for corporate deviance against owners? To the extent that large corporations are manageable by any group, it means that management could be forced to become more aggressively profit-oriented in order to attract and maintain the loyalty of institutional investors. It means that institutional investors carry big sticks, and in such a situation deviance against owners could become less probable.

In one sense, then, shifting patterns of ownership appear positive. Institutional investors could force corporations to serve their stockholders better. However, corporations have normative obligations to other groups, so the future may not be so positive. Though not happening yet, corporations in the future may be forced by institutional investors to pursue aggressively stockholder interests that violate the rights of employees, customers, and the public-at-large. We examine the first of these possibilities, corporate deviance against employees, in the next chapter.

ANNOTATED SELECTED READINGS

Berle, Adolf A., Jr., and Gardiner C. Means. *The Modern Corporation and Private Property.* New York: Macmillan, 1932. A landmark that highlighted and explained the loss of power of corporate owners to managers and that still makes interesting reading.

Burch, Philip H., Jr. *The Managerial Revolution Reassessed: Family Control in America's Large Corporations.* Lexington, MA: Lexington Books, 1972. A

well-documented but turgid attempt to show that family control of corporations still is pervasive.

Dirks, Raymond L., and Leonard Gross. *The Great Wall Street Scandal.* New
   York: McGraw-Hill, 1974. A review of the Equity Funding scandal.

Finn, David. *The Corporate Oligarch.* New York: Simon & Schuster, 1969.
   Discusses executives' freedom from accountability to stockholders (especially
   Chapter 3), in addition to other aspects of corporate life and leadership.

Soble, Ronald L., and Robert E. Dallos. *The Impossible Dream: The Equity
   Funding Story.* New York: Putnam's, 1974. A review of the Equity Funding
   scandal.

NOTES

1. David M. Phillips, "Managerial Misuse of Property: The Synthesizing
    Thread in Corporate Doctrine," *Rutgers Law Review* 32 (July 1979): 184.
2. Ibid., pp. 184–236. See also Christopher D. Stone, *Where the Law Ends*
    (New York: Harper & Row, 1975), especially Parts I, II, and V; Ralph
    Nader, Mark Green, and Joel Seligman, *Taming the Giant Corporation*
    (New York: Norton, 1976).
3. Phillips, "Managerial," 188.
4. Ibid., p. 198.
5. See Martin L. Needleman and Carolyn Needleman, "Organizational
    Crime: Two Models of Criminogenesis," *The Sociological Quarterly* 20
    (Autumn 1979): 517–520.
6. See John N. Hazard, "Soviet Property Law and Social Change," in Alex
    Inkeles and Kent Geiger, eds., *Soviet Society: A Book of Readings* (Boston:
    Houghton Mifflin, 1961), pp. 201–209.
7. Ibid., p. 209.
8. David Finn, *The Corporate Oligarch* (New York: Simon & Schuster, 1969),
    p. 53.
9. Harold E. Pepinsky, "From White Collar Crime to Exploitation: Redefini-
    tion of a Field," *The Journal of Criminal Law & Criminology* 65 (1974):
    229.
10. Emmanual Stein, *Government and the Investor* (New York: Farrar and
    Rinehart, 1941), p. 63.
11. Sidney Robbins, *The Securities Market* (New York: Free Press, 1966), p.
    106.
12. For a critical review see: Homer Kripke, *The SEC and Corporate Dis-
    closure: Regulation in Search of a Purpose* (New York: Harcourt, 1979).
13. This section is based upon Lee J. Seidler, Frederick Andrews, and Marc
    J. Epstein, eds., *The Equity Funding Papers: The Anatomy of a Fraud*

(Santa Barbara: Wiley, 1977); Ronald L. Soble and Robert E. Dallos, *The Impossible Dream: The Equity Funding Story* (New York: Putnam's, 1974); Raymond L. Dirks and Leonard Gross, *The Great Wall Street Scandal* (New York: McGraw-Hill, 1974); and William E. Blundell, "Equity Funding: 'I Did It for the Jollies,'" in John M. Johnson and Jack D. Douglas, eds., *Crime At The Top: Deviance in Business and the Professions* (Philadelphia: Lippincott, 1978), pp. 153–185.

14. Seidler, *The Equity Funding Papers,* pp. 3–4.
15. Soble and Dallos, *The Impossible Dream,* p. 48.
16. Ibid., pp. 15–17.
17. Ibid., pp. 275–276.
18. Ibid., p. 218.
19. Ibid., p. 276.
20. Dirks and Gross, *The Great Wall Street Scandal,* pp. 239–240.
21. Ibid., p. 239.
22. Soble and Dallos, *The Impossible Dream,* p. 139.
23. Seidler, *The Equity Funding Papers,* p. 8.
24. Ibid., p. 17.
25. Chapter 8 of this book discusses loyalty and whistle-blowing in detail.
26. Dirks and Gross, *The Great Wall Street Scandal,* p. 73.
27. See James S. Coleman, *Power and the Structure of Society* (New York: Norton, 1974), pp. 13–31.
28. Milton Friedman, "The Social Responsibility of Business Is to Increase Its Profits," *The Sunday Times Magazine* (September 13, 1970), p. 33.
29. Based upon Adolf A. Berle, Jr., and Gardiner C. Means, *The Modern Corporation and Private Property* (New York: Macmillan, 1932). The idea may date much earlier. Michael Harrington, for instance, states that "the famous separation of ownership and control, discovered for American social science by Berle and Means in the 1920's, was clearly recognized by Marx in Volume III of *Das Kapital* more than fifty years earlier" (*The Twilight of Capitalism* [New York: Simon & Schuster, 1976], p. 198.) This and other antecedents of Berle and Means are discussed in John Child, *The Business Enterprise in Modern Industrial Society* (London: Collier-Macmillan, 1969), p. 37.
30. See note 29.
31. Berle and Means, *The Modern Corporation,* p. 277.
32. Ibid., p. 122.
33. The preferences of management for growth, rather than for maximum profits preferred by rational stockholders, significantly alter corporate behavior. According to one economist, "numerical calculations based on statistical observation suggest that a rather growth-conscious management could typically grow almost twice as fast ... as compared to the values which would be obtained in an otherwise comparable corporation dominated by stockholders who knew all the facts." See Robin Marris, "Galbraith, Solow, and The Trust About Corporations," *Public Interest* 11 (Spring 1968): 44.

34. See Coleman, *Power,* pp. 33–54, and also Duane S. Elgin and Robert A. Bushnell, "The Limits to Complexity: Are Bureaucracies Becoming Unmanageable?" *The Futurist* (December 1977), pp. 337–349.
35. John Kenneth Galbraith, *The New Industrial State* (New York: New American Library, 1967), pp. 74–79.
36. Coleman, *Power,* p. 37.
37. The discussion that follows is based upon Marshall E. Blume and Irwin Friend, "The American Stockholder," The *Wharton Magazine* (Spring 1978); United States Senate, Committee on Government Affairs, Subcommittee on Reports, Accounting, and Management, *Voting Rights in Major Corporations: A Staff Study* (Washington, D.C.: U.S. Government Printing Office, January 1978, Stock Number 052-070-04371-7).

4

Deviance against employees

In the first place, no employer in a position of authority ever saw a sick worker or knew at firsthand the gravity of this . . . man-made disease. . . . A second cause . . . may be that policy makers failed to listen to the members of their staff actually struggling with the problem.

—*Dr. Harriet L. Hardy*[1]

Traditionally, corporations have been expected to provide employees a place of employment free of known and knowable hazards.[2] In 1970 this traditional expectation became law. The Congress passed the Occupational Safety and Health Act (Public Law 91–596, "OHSA"), which requires that employers "furnish to ... employees employment and a place of employment which are free from recognized hazards that are causing or are likely to cause death or serious physical harm to ... employees."[3]

Despite considerable tradition and recent laws protecting workers, a large number of work-related injuries, illnesses, and deaths occur each year. In the most recent year for which official figures[4] are available, "One out of every eleven private sector employees experienced a job-related non-fatal injury or illness or was killed because of hazards in the work environment."[5]

Preview of the Chapter

The purpose of this chapter is to describe and analyze corporate deviance against employees. Many examples could be chosen, ranging from failure to provide employees a reasonable wage to failure to provide a work environment free of known and knowable hazards. We have chosen the latter example with a specific focus on exposure of employees to asbestos dust.

We first will examine the hazards associated with exposure to asbestos dust. Then we will show that Johns-Manville, Pittsburgh Corning, and other asbestos manufacturers were aware of asbestos dust hazards. Lastly, we will analyze exposure of employees to avoidable work-place hazards.

In describing corporate deviance against employees, we will challenge the common argument that work-place hazards are the result of regrettable corporate ignorance and inadequate preventive technology. We will show that at least in the context of asbestos dust and two corporations, extensive evidence of hazard and preventive technology were available.

In analyzing workplace hazards, we will show that corporate concern with profit is only one explanatory factor. We will argue that the replaceability of particular workers and other noneconomic forces also help to explain corporate deviance against employees.

ASBESTOS HAZARDS

Asbestos is a remarkable and highly useful mineral.[6] It is silky and fibrous and can be spun into cloth. Its chief virtue is that it is nearly indestructible, resisting both chemical action and fire. Early Romans used asbestos sacks for the dead during cremation because crematory flames reduced the body to ashes while the asbestos sack remained intact, permitting easy collection of the ashes.

Because asbestos is essentially indestructible and because it mixes easily with other substances, modern uses of it include much more than crematory sacks. Asbestos has been used as insulation and fireproofing, and for brake linings and clutch facings in automobiles. It also has been used to coat pipes and bulkheads in ships and as an ingredient in fire-fighting suits, paper, felt, millboard, floor tile, cement, plastic, paints, sealants, and in the lining of hand-held hair dryers. Consequently, "there is no factory or home without asbestos products, and there are few lungs that are not exposed to microscopic asbestos fiber."[7]

The problem with asbestos fibers in the lungs is that they are as indestructible inside the body as out. And once inside the lung, they are rarely exhaled, with most remaining in the body until death.[8] The specific problems associated with even moderate inhalation of asbestos fibers are three frequently fatal diseases: asbestosis, lung cancer, and mesothelioma.

Asbestosis[9]

Asbestosis is a frequently fatal lung disease caused by repeated inhalation of asbestos fibers. The body is unable to destroy or exhale asbestos fibers, so it reacts to their presence by isolating them. Scar tissue surrounds asbestos fibers in the lungs, making the lungs smaller and less flexible than normal. Breathing capacity, therefore, is reduced, forcing the heart to pump more blood containing less oxygen.

For the worker with advanced asbestosis, the prognosis is poor, as the lungs literally fill with strands of scar tissue. Ultimately, asbestosis causes death because there is no treatment for the disease.

Lung Cancer[10]

Cancer is the second leading cause of death in the United States, with lung cancer increasing more rapidly than any other type. Each year approximately 100,000 new cases of lung cancer are detected. The prognosis for lung cancer is even poorer than for asbestosis. Untreated, half of all lung cancer victims die within five months. With frequently debilitating medical treatment, most lung cancer victims live no longer than twelve months from the time the disease is first diagnosed. Only 5 to 10 percent of lung cancer victims are cured, showing no symptoms for a minimum of two years.

The largest single factor responsible for the current lung cancer epidemic is cigarette smoking. It is estimated that cigarette smoking causes one in four lung cancer deaths.[11] However, other factors play a role in lung cancer deaths, asbestos fibers among them. In 1964, Irving Selikoff, Jacob Churg, and E. Cutler Hammond found that lung cancer rates among building insulators, workers lightly and intermittently exposed to asbestos dust, were significantly higher than among similar persons in the general population, with the effects of cigarette smoking taken into consideration:

> Even if *all* our asbestos workers had smoked a pack of cigarettes a day (and, indeed, from our sample we know they did not), and if exposure to asbestos were of no significance, then their lung cancer death rate would have been about 3.4 times as high as the rate in the general U.S. male population. Clearly, the smoking habits of the asbestos workers cannot account for the fact that their lung cancer death rate was 6.8 times as high as that of white males in the general population.[12]

In 1978 a similar conclusion was reached by another group of re-search physicians. Their concern was with the markedly higher inci-dence of lung cancer among people who had been employed in shipyards during World War II. Despite the fact that these people also were lightly and intermittently exposed to asbestos dust for relatively short periods, most for under four years, shipyard employees showed significantly higher rates of lung cancer, with the effects of cigarette smoking controlled.[13]

Most recently, the National Cancer Institute (NCI) combined these and other studies with estimates of the total number of people exposed to asbestos fibers in their work environments. The NCI used these data to predict that "the major public health impact of asbestos-related cancer is just beginning to be reflected in overall cancer statistics."[14] Its prediction is that over two million people will die from asbestos-caused lung and other cancers.[15]

Mesothelioma[16]

The third fatal disease caused by exposure to asbestos dust is mesotheli-oma, an extremely rare form of cancer responsible for one out of every 10,000 deaths in the general population. Mesothelioma lodges in the thin membranes of the chest and abdomen. These membranes lubri-cate the lungs and intestines, allowing them to move without friction. Dr. Maxwell Borow described how mesothelioma affects these mem-branes and the organs they normally lubricate:

it starts out . . . in the abdominal cavity . . . you'll see tiny nodules—they look like tapioca pudding nodules—will be studding the peritoneum, both the abdominal wall and a different organ, the liver, the intestines. And these patients usually come to the attention of the doctor by virtue of a fluid—these little nodules secrete a fluid and these people come in with extended abdomens. Then as the disease progresses, these nodules get larger, then coalesce and start forming solid masses. When you cut through it, this big mass-like tumor—there are the organs embedded inside. They are not invaded, particularly, they're crushed. They're all crushed by virtue of this big mass, as if you had poured in cement.[17]

There is no cure for mesothelioma, and it cannot be removed surgically.[18] It kills quickly, usually within six months. There is but a single known cause of mesothelioma, exposure to asbestos dust, and those so exposed get it independent of their smoking habits.[19]

JOHNS-MANVILLE, PITTSBURGH CORNING, AND ASBESTOS DUST

Johns-Manville is the largest asbestos products manufacturer in the United States.[20] It operates fifty-five asbestos factories employing over 31,000 people. The largest of these is in Manville, New Jersey, a company town thirty-seven miles southwest of New York City. In Manville over 2,000 of the 15,000 residents are employed in the asbestos products factory, and many others are their dependents.

Asbestos product manufacturing is a profitable business. In 1978, Johns-Manville reported sales of $1.6 billion and earnings of $121.6 million. Asbestos products accounted for only 7 percent of sales but fully 19 percent of operating income.[21]

There are, of course, other asbestos manufacturers. From 1962 to 1972, PPG Industries and Corning Glass Works jointly operated an asbestos products manufacturing plant in Tyler, Texas. Compared to the Johns-Manville factory in Manville, the Tyler plant was small. At any one time it employed no more than seventy people.[22] However, it employed 895 people during twelve years that it produced asbestos products because the work caused turnover to be extremely high.

What drove people away was the dust. The very qualities that make it possible to weave asbestos or to mix it easily with other substances, its silky and fibrous texture, also cause its basic health liabilities. When manufactured dry in the absence of a low pressure vacuum system, asbestos gives off large amounts of dust.

Dust Levels at Manville

Workers at the Johns-Manville factory in Manville reported that asbestos dust levels inside the factory in the 1960s were extremely high. One employee recalled:

> There were times when the air was so thick with asbestos dust in some places that you couldn't even see. Sometimes it was even impossible to breathe with a respirator because the filters would get so clogged with asbestos.[23]

Measurements of asbestos dust levels were made by Johns-Manville, and the results of some of these measurements now have been made public.[24] Table 4.1 shows the asbestos fiber counts at representative Johns-Manville work stations by year and percent of work stations. In order to make these data usable, it is necessary first to explain the importance of fiber counts.

TABLE 4.1.   Asbestos Fiber Counts at Representative Johns-Manville Work Stations, by Year and Percent of Work Stations

YEAR	% OF WORK STATIONS WITH FIBER COUNTS OF:			
	<2	2–5	6–12	>12
1965	15.6	24.8	51.3	8.3
1967	9.8	13.7	25.5	51.0
1971	14.0	27.2	43.9	14.9
1972	91.0	9.0	0	0

Source: Bruce Porter, "An Asbestos Town Struggles With a Killer," *Saturday Review of the Society* 1 (February 17, 1973), p. 31. Copyright © 1973 by Saturday Review. All rights reserved. Reprinted by permission.

The fiber count measures the number of fibers of at least a given length found in a given space. More specifically, it is the number of asbestos fibers longer than five microns that are found in a cubic centimeter of air. A cubic centimeter is roughly the size of a small thimble, and five microns is five millionths of a meter. An asbestos fiber five microns or longer is visible by using a standard optical microscope.

Fiber counts are used to specify the level at which exposure causes asbestosis, lung cancer, and mesothelioma. Although these "threshold values" are not precisely known, some scientists are beginning to suggest that there is no safe level of exposure, and there exists essential scientific agreement that a fiber count greater than two constitutes a severe danger to the persons so exposed. Dr. Irving Selikoff, for example, estimated that for workers exposed to a fiber count of five for forty years, 85 percent would develop asbestosis, 20 percent would have lung cancer, and 7 percent should develop mesothelioma;[25] none would escape their work experience healthy. Asbestos fiber counts are thus a way of predicting deaths due to exposure to asbestos dust.

Data in Table 4.1 show that Johns-Manville employees were exposed to asbestos dust levels we now know are extremely hazardous. Prior to 1972, employees at approximately 85 percent of Johns-Manville work stations were exposed to fiber counts greater than two. However, the situation then changed dramatically. Between 1971 and 1972, the percentage of work stations exceeding the two-fiber standard dropped from 86 percent to 9 percent.

This is a remarkable improvement, and the reasons for it deserve mention. When Congress passed the Occupational Safety and Health Act in June of 1970, OSHA was given the power to limit exposure to hazardous substances. Asbestos then was recognized as an extremely hazardous substance, and the new agency gave first priority to setting mandatory asbestos exposure standards.

The single most frequently advanced standard by persons outside the asbestos industry was a fiber count of two. Persons representing the asbestos industry responded to the proposed two-fiber standard by arguing that it could not be achieved without enormous financial investment. Henry B. Moreno, a senior vice-president for Johns-Manville, argued early in 1972:

> For us to achieve a standard of two fibers per cubic centimeter would require capital expenditures of twelve million dollars, and additional operating costs of five million dollars per year.... For these reasons, we believe that it would be nothing less than complete social irresponsibility to adopt a two-fiber standard for occupational exposure to asbestos ...[26]

Industry objections were considered when OSHA issued its asbestos standard in June of 1972. Until July 1, 1976, asbestos employees legally could be exposed to five fibers per cubic centimeter, despite the known risks. Then the maximum exposure level would drop to two.

By the end of 1972, however, nearly all work stations at the Manville plant already were benefiting from a fiber count no higher than two. Thus, by 1972 it already was possible for industry using existing technology to lower asbestos dust levels significantly and quickly. It took less than a year.

Dust Levels at Tyler

Conditions at the Pittsburgh Corning Plant in Tyler, Texas, are now known to have been even more hazardous that at Johns-Manville. One employee recalled:

> When I think back, all I can remember is the dust. Why, most of the time I worked there you couldn't see from one end of the place to the other— especially when there was any sunlight coming through the windows.[27]

Added to employee reports are those of government officials. In October of 1971, officials of the National Institute of Occupational Safety and Health (NIOSH) conducted an industrial hygiene and medical survey of the Tyler factory. One of the NIOSH physicians, William Johnson, was shocked by what he saw:

> The place was an unholy mess. . . . A thick layer of dust coated everything —from floors, ceilings, and rafters to drinking fountains. As we walked through the interior, we saw men forking asbestos fiber into a feeding machine as if it were hay. They obviously had no idea of the hazard involved.[28]

Hard data for the Tyler plant also are available, thanks to six surveys of dust levels taken there between 1963 and October of 1972.[29] The last survey was part of a NIOSH industrial hygiene study of the Tyler plant.[30] The NIOSH findings reported in Table 4.2 show that dust levels were dangerously high. In the *least* dusty work station in the factory, inspection/packing, the average asbestos dusty level was four times the 1972 OSHA standard and more than ten times the 1976 standard.

TABLE 4.2.   Average and Maximum Number of Asbestos Fibers Longer Than Five Microns Per Cubic Centimeter of Air at the Tyler, Texas, Asbestos Factory in October of 1972 by Department

DEPARTMENT	AVERAGE NUMBER OF FIBERS/ CUBIC CENTIMETER	MAXIMUM NUMBER OF FIBERS/ CUBIC CENTIMETER
Mixing	75	185
Forming	39	134
Finishing	41	208
Inspection/Packing	23	92

Adapted from Paul Brodeur, *Expendable Americans* (New York: The Viking Press, 1974), p. 50.

CORPORATE AWARENESS OF ASBESTOS HAZARDS

This section establishes that Johns-Manville, Pittsburgh Corning, and other asbestos manufacturers[31] were aware of the hazards of asbestos dust. To establish this point, we first will examine public evidence of linkages between asbestos dust and employee illness and deaths. Then we will review recently released corporate memos and documents.

Public Evidence of Linkages

Public evidence of linkages between asbestos dust and pulmonary incapacitation date back to the first century. Pliny (23–79 A.D.), a Roman naturalist and writer, reported that the asbestos miners who mined asbestos for crematory robes wore crude respirators in an effort to minimize inhalation of the intense dust characteristic of their work.[32]

The first distinctly modern linkage of asbestos dust with death was in England in 1907. By 1928 firm linkages had been established in English medical journals.[33] English physician Donald Hunter summarized the English experience linking asbestos dust and death as follows:

> The first case of asbestosis known in Great Britain was observed in 1900 and described by Murray in 1907. The man had worked on a carding machine for fourteen years and was the last survivor of ten men who had worked in the card room, the others having died about the age of thirty with lung disease. He died ... at the age of thirty-four, and necropsy [autopsy] revealed extensive diffuse pulmonary fibrosis ... the lungs were found to contain asbestosis bodies. ... Difficulties of certification delayed further action and cases of asbestosis continued to occur. Real attention was drawn to the disease by Cook (1924). But it was the case published by Seiler (1928) which seemed to establish an unequivocal relationship between asbestos and pulmonary fibrosis. ...[34]

Numerous reports of the hazards of asbestos dust were being reported in British, American, and German medical journals.[35] These reports were available to anyone who might have been interested. In fact, the earliest were available when Henry Johns and Thomas Manville opened their asbestos products factory in Manville, New Jersey, in 1912.

Some in the corporate sector and outside took notice of these early reports. Insurance companies are vitally interested in mortality figures and in identifying the factors that cause death. By 1918 they had decided that it was too expensive and risky to insure asbestos workers. Specifically, "American and Canadian insurance companies were ... declining to insure asbestos workers because of the assumed hazardous conditions of the asbestos industry."[36] And by 1918 four states, Iowa, Illinois, Hawaii, and California, already had enacted workmen's compensation laws including the disease of asbestosis.[37]

Across the next thirty years numerous additional articles and books appeared. In 1935 two research physicians published an article linking asbestos dust with asbestosis, lung cancer, and mesothelioma in *The American Journal of Cancer*.[38] In 1955 a book published by Little, Brown and Company, then as now well-known and respected publishing house, provided clear description of how asbestos diseases and deaths could be prevented.[39] And in 1964 a now classic paper by physician Irving Selikoff and colleagues established that workers lightly and intermittently exposed to asbestos experienced significantly higher death rates.[40]

Since 1964 a series of papers in medical journals and books have been devoted to asbestos diseases.[41] Some of these reports are about people who worked with asbestos materials for very short periods and still contracted asbestos diseases. These more recent studies confirm what was first reported in 1907 by an English physician: exposure to asbestos dust is extremely hazardous.

Corporate Memos and Documents

Across the past few years asbestos workers and handlers have brought a series of lawsuits against Johns-Manville, Pittsburgh Corning, and other asbestos manufacturers. These suits have produced approximately 150 pages of previously unavailable corporate memos and documents.

In essence these corporate memos and documents include

1. Letters and files going back to 1934 from two of the biggest asbestos firms, Johns-Manville and Raybestos-Manhattan, noting efforts by senior executives of those companies to suppress information about the potential harm to workers from asbestos ... executives were allowed to edit out or tone down reference to asbestos-caused disease in industry-supported research studies.
2. Documents and statements from former asbestos officials that the industry spent thousands of dollars setting up research projects at a Saranac Lake, New York, laboratory in the 1930s and 1940s and then prevented the researchers from publishing findings indicating possible asbestos danger to humans.

3. Documents indicating that another large asbestos manufacturer, the Philip Carey Co., ignored warnings from the firm's own medical consultant . . . and then dropped him as a consultant after he warned of possible lawsuits from workers exposed to asbestos.

4. Corporate files showing that asbestos companies quietly settled injury and death claims from workers who handled asbestos products years before the companies and the asbestos industry acknowledged that asbestos could cause serious harm to workers.

5. Additional files and testimony from former asbestos officials that Johns-Manville . . . apparently maintained a policy into the 1970s of not telling its employees that their physical examinations showed signs of asbestosis. This policy was maintained despite the industry's acknowledgment years earlier of the danger of the disease and despite the awareness by company executives that it is progressive and fatal unless caught and treated in its early stages.[42]

In sum: public evidence and corporate memos and documents establish that Johns-Manville, Pittsburgh Corning, and other asbestos manufacturers were aware of the hazards of asbestos dust.

ANALYSIS OF CORPORATE DEVIANCE AGAINST EMPLOYEES

Many traditional analyses of corporate deviance against employees emphasize the role of profit in a capitalist economic system. In 1906, for example, forty-six employees were killed at the United States Steel Corporation plant in Chicago. A young observer, William Hard, was quick to isolate profit maximization as the most important reason for these deaths, noting that "figures that indicate products and profits are the only figures handled and scrutinized"[43] by corporate elites.

Many contemporary analyses also place primary emphasis on the role of profit.[44] Sheldon Samuels, an occupational health and safety expert for the AFL-CIO, put the contemporary version of the traditional argument in an especially forceful manner:

The economics of the situation are very simple. . . Even if all the identifiable costs were placed on the employer we cannot always be sure that it would not be cheaper for the employer to replace dead workers than to keep them alive. It may even be profitable, if only dollars and cents are counted . . . to sacrifice a life that has already achieved peak productivity.[45]

Short-Term Profits

Such analyses are consistent with the asbestos experience. In 1972, Johns-Manville estimated it would cost $12 million to install dust control equipment and an additional $5 million to operate and maintain that equipment.[46] In the three years preceding 1972, Workmen's Compensation payments for employees disabled or killed by asbestos dust averaged only $1 million per year, making them less expensive than dust control equipment.

However, profit is not the only reason executives ignore or suppress evidence of hazard. Corporate structure causes executives to make decisions that result in employee illnesses and deaths, and the federal government contributes to corporate actions contrary to the best interests of employees.

Corporate Structure

Corporate structure encourages decisions that result in employee illnesses and fatalities. Corporations (1) reward executives for short-term successes, (2) do not penalize executives for long-term failures, and (3) shield executives from responsibility for, and awareness of, illnesses and fatalities.

Corporate Rewards

Corporate executives are expected to perform well along a number of dimensions. Evaluation of performance, however, generally is limited to short-term goals, as with production or profit figures.[47] Joseph L. Bowers summarizes the rewards available to executives in most corporations:

> The central source of motivation, the career system, is so designed that virtually all measures are short-run and internally focused. [Executives] are rewarded for performance but performance is almost always defined as short-run economic or technical results. The more objective the system, the more an attempt is made to quantify results, the harder it is to broaden the rules of the game to take into account the social role of the executive.[48]

For asbestos executives facing a choice between relatively inexpensive compensation payments and considerably more expensive control equipment, career rewards provide clear decision-making criteria. Equipment intended to prevent or control work-place hazards reduces productivity. It generally adds steps to the production process and may require that employees utilize uncomfortable safety equipment. Additionally, safety equipment ultimately reduces a factory or division's profits. In the short term, executives best serve their careers by minimizing these costs.

Corporate Sanctions

Rarely are executives sanctioned for long-term failures. It generally is recognized that calculation of the long-term costs of a particular decision is extremely difficult.[49] As time passes, the number of factors that can play upon a decision increases, often unpredictably. What once was a short-term success can years later become a serious blunder.

Asbestos executives made decisions that recently have proved to be long-term blunders. They specifically failed to anticipate emergence of expensive personal injury and class-action suits. In January of 1970, for example, more than 400 former Tyler employees filed a personal injury suit against their employers, some South African and British suppliers of asbestos, and the federal government.[50] The workers charged that they never were warned of the hazard of asbestos exposure. In February of 1978, their suit was settled out of court for $20 million. And in October of 1978 more than 5,000 former and current shipyard employees filed a $1 billion lawsuit in Los Angeles.[51] Their suit charges that Johns-Manville and other leading asbestos manufacturers knew as early as 1934 that exposure to asbestos dust causes asbestosis, lung cancer, mesothelioma, and other cancers, but conspired to hide these hazards. The suit seeks all of the profits made since 1934 by Johns-Manville and other leading asbestos products manufacturers.

In addition to class-action suits brought by groups of employees, there has been an enormous increase in suits brought by individual plaintiffs. In 1976 there were 159 new lawsuits filed against Johns-Manville, in 1978 there were 792, and filings for the first four months of 1979 suggested a year-end total of almost 1,600. The average cost per settlement in 1978 was $15,400.[52] If only half of the 1,600 suits filed in 1979 are settled in favor of plaintiffs and assuming the average settlement remains $15,400, then settlement costs will amount to over $12 million just for individual plaintiffs.

The reason why executives are not sanctioned is quite straightforward. As was true of asbestos decisions, there frequently is such a gap between decision and consequence that corporations find it difficult, if not impossible, to sanction executives responsible for long-term blunders. Executives who make these decisions are promoted, retired, or dead, which makes them invulnerable to corporate penalties. Others, therefore, pick up the pieces left in the wake of serious mistakes.

Executives Are Shielded

Corporate structure shields executives from responsibility for, and awareness of, illnesses and fatalities. Role specialization makes company physicians responsible for illnesses and fatalities. Corporate hierarchy and size make employee illnesses and deaths silent events. Company doctors do little to break this silence.

Almost all large corporations and many smaller ones employ company physicians. These physicians frequently give routine physical examinations to employees. And if they actually work at a corporation's production facilities, their presence can mean the difference between life and death in the first few moments following a serious industrial accident.

Company physicians should be no less important in the context of occupational illnesses. They, more than anyone else, should be the first to learn of newly published links between industrial substances and illnesses. Moreover, in the course of their physical examinations of employees, they should discover the peculiar hazards of their industry. Role specialization makes company physicians responsible for occupational illnesses and the fatalities such illnesses can cause.

Company physicians generally have done little to prevent or control work-related illness and fatalities. In fact, their actions often have been destructive of human health and life. Consider physician Lee Grant, medical director of PPG Industries from 1963 to 1972, when PPG and Corning jointly owned the Tyler plant. Dr. Grant certainly should have read the many papers and books linking asbestos dust with illness and death. Additionally, Dr. Grant received reports of unsafe asbestos dust levels at the Tyler factory and made several personal visits there.

His response to the research and reports was to lie often and sometimes well. Dr. Grant lied to the plant manager and employees about the effects of exposure to asbestos dust,[53] to union officials about safety precautions,[54] and to government officials about dust levels at the Tyler plant.[55] He was not the only corporate official who lied. Considering his pivotal position, however, it would seem that Dr. Grant's lies were among the most important.

Also consider the actions of Kenneth Wallace Smith, former Johns-Manville medical director. Johns-Manville maintained a policy of not informing employees that their routine physical examinations revealed asbestosis,[56] a policy developed and supported by Dr. Smith. In 1949 he explained his actions:

> Eventually, compensation will be paid to each of those men. But, as long as a man is not disabled it is felt he should not be told of his condition so that he can live and work in peace and the company can benefit by his many years of experience.[57]

The actions and motivations of Drs. Grant and Smith are not unique among company physicians. Essentially similar actions have been undertaken by company physicians employed by firms such as Dow Chemical,[58] Kawecki Berylco Industries,[59] Standard Oil of Indiana,[60] Bethlehem Steel,[61] American Smelting and Refining Company,[62] Anaconda,[63] Union Carbide,[64] Minnesota Mining and Manufacturing,[65] FMC Corporation,[66] Chrysler,[67] Ford,[68] Midland Steel,[69] and the National Lead Company.[70] The list is longer,[71] but the point is this: company physicians routinely use their pivotal positions to protect corporate interests against the interests of employees. They are company doctors, with their first loyalty to their employers.

Silent Illnesses and Deaths

It is not unusual for contemporary students of the work experience to describe employees as machines.[72] And it is not unusual for employees to describe themselves as machines.[73] These descriptions and feelings are important in explaining the decisions of corporate executives. To compare an employee to a machine is to suggest that employees are unimportant except insofar as they contribute to production. Machines are replaceable, and one hardly becomes attached to something so easily replaced.

The sheer size of many corporations increases the marginal position of employees. In a large corporation top-level executives do not know individual workers. They do not know them as people with dreams and hopes, disappointments and fears. Employees also are unknowable. Corporate elites have neither the time nor the interest to know and know about employees directly involved in production.

Furthermore, with a large and sometimes desperate reserve labor force, particular employees are replaceable. As particular employees become disabled and die, others easily and quickly take their places. Employees come and go, and the corporation and its executives are unaffected.

From the perspective of corporate elites, illnesses and fatalities are silent events.[74] Victims are not known or known about. Corporate elites rarely see sick workers. They do not experience the terror and sometimes the anger associated with disablement and death, witness the tears and fear of a dead worker's family, or attend a dead worker's funeral. Corporate hierarchy shields executives from the consequences of their decisions.

The Federal Government

Corporate structure is not the sole source of deviance against asbestos employees. The federal government also has contributed by its failure to exercise the health- and lifesaving powers only it possesses. And it may expand its contribution by indemnifying deviant corporations, pulling them back from the brink of serious financial trouble.

Federal Inaction

When a known work hazard in an industry is expensive to correct, any single firm probably will not decide unilaterally to eliminate it. Such unilateral provision of safe working conditions would increase cost to the firm but not to its competitors, putting the firm at an avoidable disadvantage. For similar reasons, no single state is likely to force its corporations unilaterally to provide a safe work environment. Unilateral state action invites corporate flight and ensures that new factories will be located in other states and countries.[75]

In the context of asbestos dust and other hazardous substances,[76] the federal government repeatedly has been slow to take effective action. A variety of governmental agents and agencies surveyed the Pittsburgh Corning and Johns-Manville plants.[77] These agents and agencies possessed information that asbestos dust levels were above those identified as causing death. Not until December of 1971, however, did the federal government take action. Using the emergency powers of the OSHAct, Secretary of Labor James Hodgson issued an emergency standard of five fibers longer than five microns per cubic centimeter of air.[78] In June of 1972 he again acted, extending the five-fiber standard until July 1, 1976, when it was lowered to two fibers.

The effects of these long overdue actions were clear. Pittsburgh Corning responded to Secretary Hodgson's emergency asbestos standard by closing its Tyler, Texas, factory.[79] It had been an economically marginal operation, profitable only as long as the company could continue to expose its employees to asbestos dust. Federal action forced it to stop causing illnesses and fatalities.

At Johns-Manville, despite vigorous opposition to stricter standards, dust levels dropped dramatically once they were announced (see Table 4.1). According to estimates advanced by research physicians, the federal action would produce approximately thirty fewer deaths per one hundred Johns-Manville employees.[80] Although belated and perhaps inadequate, federal action did help protect employees.

Federal Indemnification

Because of numerous unanticipated lawsuits, Johns-Manville is on the brink of serious financial trouble. Stephen Solomon of *Fortune* has noted that "the wave of claims could mount up the next two decades, exhausting . . . insurance coverage and causing a serious drain on the company's reserves."[81]

Although troubling to the company, these lawsuits and the financial injury they can cause have two positive effects. The first is specific deterrence, the hypothetical omission of an act in the future because of having been sanctioned for that same act in the past.[82] Being threatened with paying, and actually having to pay, large amounts of money should serve to make Johns-Manville and other financially troubled asbestos manufacturers more cautious in the context of future decisions affecting work-place safety.

A second positive effect of lawsuits and financial injury is general deterrence, the hypothesized omission of an act because of awareness that others have been punished for the same or similar activities.[83] Johns-Manville's financial trouble presumably warns other corporations of the long-term consequences of decisions to expose employees to hazardous substances. Having seen what is happening and what might happen to Johns-Manville, other corporations should take similar actions less frequently.

Federal indemnification of Johns-Manville and other asbestos manufacturers obviously would negate these deterrent effects. If the federal government pays for the injuries and deaths attributable to asbestos manufacturers, then asbestos manufacturers have less reason to avoid similar actions in the future. Equally, corporations in other industries have less reason to attempt to examine the long-term consequences of their decisions. Federal indemnification eliminates the hypothesized specific and general deterrence associated with lawsuits and subsequent financial injury.

Nevertheless, on August 2, 1977, Congressperson Millicient Fenwick (Republican, New Jersey) introduced the "Asbestos Health Hazards Compensation Act" (H.R. 8689).[84] This bill would compensate victims of asbestos diseases by using corporate, union, tobacco industry, and government funds. The federal government would pay half of all costs, with its commitment open-ended should funds from other sources be inadequate.[85] All other forms of compensation, including lawsuits against asbestos manufacturers, would be prohibited.

Johns-Manville is an enthusiastic supporter of the Asbestos Health Hazards Compensation Act. The company should enthusiastically support the bill. It helped write it, [86] something Representative Fenwick, whose home district includes Manville, New Jersey, freely admits.

The prospects for the passage of Representative Fenwick's bill are uncertain. Since its introduction only scattered hearings have been held, and, in these hearings, the bill received mixed reception.[87] However, opposition to protecting asbestos manufacturers has not been the cause of the bill's problems. Opposition and delay have come from those who would indemnify *all* corporations from the costs associated with exposure of employees to hazardous substances.[88] The prospects for this comprehensive approach, a blanket indemnification of corporations, appears more certain than those for Representative Fenwick's and Johns-Manville's bill alone. Such indemnification by the federal government would free corporations from financial responsibility for avoidable work-related illnesses and deaths.

SUMMARY

By tradition and recently by law, employees have a right to a work environment free of known and knowable hazards. Although standards frequently are vague and almost always subject to change, it generally is recognized that when evidence of hazard and adequate preventive technology are available, employees should not be injured, made ill, or killed by their work.

Description of the actions of Johns-Manville and PPG Industries suggested that they needlessly exposed their employees to asbestos dust. Dust levels were extremely high even though awareness of hazard and adequate preventive technology were both available.

Analysis of these actions suggested that several factors were important. Traditional explanations emphasizing corporate concerns with short-term profits were found to be consistent with the asbestos experience. However, profit was not the only reason asbestos manufacturers ignored or suppressed evidence of hazard. It was found that corporate structure and the federal government also contribute to actions contrary to the best interests of employees.

ANNOTATED SELECTED READINGS

Blot, William J. "Lung Cancer After Employment in Shipyards During World War II." *The New England Journal of Medicine* 299 (September 21, 1978): 620–624. Easily readable history of exceptionally high lung cancer rates among male residents of coastal Georgia. Traces the problem of shipyard exposures to low levels of asbestos dust.

Brodeur, Paul. *Expendable Americans.* New York: Viking, 1974. A well-researched and occasionally angry analysis of corporate deviance against employees, with a focus on asbestos and the Tyler plant.

Hamilton, Alice. *Exploring the Dangerous Trades.* Boston: Little, Brown, 1943. An early and excellent analysis of corporate exposure of employees to hazardous conditions and substances.

Hardy, Harriet. "Beryllium Poisoning—Lessons in Control of Man-made disease." *The New England Journal of Medicine* 273 (November 25, 1965): 1188–1199. Traces history of preventable occupational disease, giving special attention to beryllium poisoning.

Swartz, Joel. "Silent Killers at Work." In M. David Ermann and Richard J. Lundman, eds., *Corporate and Governmental Deviance.* New York: Oxford U.P., 1978. Pp. 114–128. Discussion and analysis of "corporate homicide" with explanatory attention directed at the capitalist system of production.

U.S. Department of Labor, Bureau of Labor Statistics. *Occupational Injuries and Illnesses in the United States, 1975.* Washington, DC: U.S. Government Printing Office, 1978, Bulletin #1981. Counts of injuries, illnesses, and deaths reported to Bureau of Labor Statistics by private sector employers. Although it tends to underestimate, it is an excellent starting point. Updated irregularly, so check for most recent issue.

NOTES

1. Harriet Hardy, "Beryllium Poisoning—Lessons in Control of Man-made Disease," *The New England Journal of Medicine* 273 (November 25, 1965), p. 1197.
2. Ibid., pp. 1188–1191. Dr. Hardy emphasizes that it was not until the early 1920s that a clear concern with employee safety and health emerged.
3. The Occupational Safety and Health Act of 1970 (Public Law 91–596) Sec. 5 (a), p. 4. Hereafter called OSHAct of 1970.

4. U.S. Department of Labor, Bureau of Labor Statistics, *Occupational Injuries and Illnesses in the United States,* 1975 (Washington, DC: U.S. Government Printing Office, 1978, Bulletin #1981).
5. Ibid., p. 1.
6. The material on asbestos as a product is from Donald Hunter, *The Diseases of Occupations* (Boston: Little, Brown, 1955), pp. 874–875.
7. Joseph A. Page and Mary-Win O'Brien, *Bitter Wages: Ralph Nader's Study Group Report on Disease and Injury on the Job* (New York: Grossman Publishers, 1973), p. 21.
8. Jeanne M. Stellman and Susan M. Daum, *Work Is Dangerous to Your Health* (New York: Random House, 1973), p. 172.
9. The discussion of asbestosis is from Morton M. Ziskind, "Occupational Pulmonary Disease," *Clinical Symposia* 30 (1978):12–13.
10. The discussion of lung cancer is from John M. Merrill, "Lung Cancer," *Medical Challenge* (October 1978):23–25.
11. Ibid., p. 23.
12. Irving J. Selikoff, Jacob Churg, and E. Cutler Hammond, "Asbestos Exposures and Neoplasia," *Journal of the American Medical Association* 22 (April 1964):145.
13. William Blot, Jr., "Lung Cancer After Employment in Shipyards During World War II," *The New England Journal of Medicine* 299 (September 21, 1978), p. 621.
14. Cited by Stephen Solomon, "The Asbestos Fallout at Johns-Manville," *Fortune* 99 (May 7, 1979), p. 198.
15. Ibid., p. 198.
16. This discussion of mesothelioma is based upon Bruce Porter, "An Asbestos Town Struggles with a Killer," *Saturday Review of the Society* 1 (February 17, 1973), p. 26, and Stellman and Daum, *Work,* p. 173.
17. From Rachel Scott, *Muscle and Blood* (New York: Dutton, 1974), pp. 197–198.
18. Porter, "Asbestos Town," p. 29.
19. Stellman and Daum, *Work,* p. 173.
20. Porter, "Asbestos Town," p. 28.
21. Solomon, "The Asbestos Fallout," p. 197.
22. Paul Brodeur, *Expendable Americans* (New York: Viking, 1974).
23. Porter, "Asbestos Town," p. 29.
24. Ibid., p. 31.
25. Brodeur, *Expendable Americans,* p. 146.
26. Ibid., p. 128.
27. Ibid., p. 85.
28. Ibid., p. 48.
29. Ibid., pp. 11, 19, and 26.
30. Ibid., p. 50.
31. See Kenneth W. Carlson, Prepared statement for U.S. House of Representatives, Committee on Education and Labor, Subcommittee on Compensation, Health and Safety, *Hearings: Asbestos-Related Occupational*

Diseases, 95th Congress, Second Session (U.S. Government Printing Office, Washington, D.C., 1979), pp. 25–52.
32. Hunter, *The Diseases,* pp. 874–875.
33. Ibid., p. 877.
34. Ibid., p. 879.
35. Ibid., pp. 874–875; Carlson, Prepared statement, pp. 25–52.
36. Brodeur, *Expendable Americans,* p. 6.
37. Carlson, Prepared statement, p. 25.
38. Kenneth M. Lynch and W. Atman Smith, "Pulmonary Asbestosis," *The American Journal of Cancer* 24 (May 1935): 56–64.
39. Hunter, *The Diseases,* pp. 874–885.
40. Selikoff et al., "Asbestos Exposures."
41. See Blot, "Lung Cancer," for an example as well as citations to more recent literature.
42. Bill Richards, "New Data on Asbestos Indicate Cover-up of Effects on Workers," *The Washington Post,* Section A, 12 November 1978, pp. 1, 6. Portions have been reprinted in *Asbestos-Related Occupational Diseases,* which is available in library systems with a government-documents depository or by writing your congressperson and asking for a copy. See note 31 for a complete title.
43. Quoted in Scott, *Muscle and Blood,* p. 43.
44. For example, Joel Swartz, "Silent Killers at Work," in M. David Ermann and Richard J. Lundman, eds., *Corporate and Governmental Deviance* (New York: Oxford U.P., 1978), p. 115.
45. Quoted in Brodeur, *Expendable Americans,* p. 207.
46. Ibid., p. 128.
47. Rosabeth Moss Kanter, *Men and Women of the Corporation* (New York: Basic Books, 1977), pp. 53–54.
48. Joseph L. Bowers, "On the Amoral Organization," in Robin Morris, ed., *The Corporate Society* (New York: Wiley, 1967), pp. 202–203.
49. Kanter, *Men and Women,* p. 53.
50. "Asbestos-Dust Suit Settled," *Columbus Dispatch,* Section A, 9 February 1978, p. 3.
51. "5,000 File $1 Billion Suit Against Asbestos Makers," *Columbus Dispatch,* Section A, 29 October 1978, p. 9.
52. Solomon, "The Asbestos Fallout," p. 198.
53. Brodeur, *Expendable Americans,* p. 48.
54. Ibid., p. 60.
55. Ibid., p. 54.
56. Richards, "New Data," Section A, p. 6.
57. Quoted in ibid.
58. Brodeur, *Expendable Americans,* p. 139.
59. Hardy, "Beryllium Poisoning," p. 1196. For an identification of the corporation, see Scott, *Muscle and Blood,* pp. 5–36.
60. Swartz, "Silent Killers," p. 121.
61. Scott, *Muscle and Blood,* p. 45.

62. Ibid., p. 65.
63. Ibid., p. 76.
64. Ibid., p. 80.
65. Ibid., p. 87.
66. Ibid., p. 99.
67. Ibid., p. 131.
68. Ibid., p. 143.
69. Page and O'Brien, *Bitter Wages,* p. 3.
70. Ibid., p. 31.
71. Ray Davidson, *Peril on the Job* (Washington, D.C.: Public Affairs Press, 1970), pp. 138–150.
72. Rosabeth Moss Kanter and Barry Stein, eds., *Life in Organizations: Workplaces as People Experience Them* (New York: Basic Books, 1979), pp. 176–190.
73. Studs Terkel, *Working* (New York: Avon Books, 1975), especially pp. 221–265.
74. Based upon Hardy, "Beryllium Poisoning," p. 1197.
75. Brodeur, *Expendable Americans,* pp. 152–153.
76. For examples see H. Peter Metzger, *The Atomic Establishment* (New York: Simon & Schuster, 1972); Davidson, *Peril.*
77. See Brodeur, *Expendable Americans,* pp. 11, 19, 26, 27, and 50.
78. Porter, "Asbestos Town," p. 31.
79. Brodeur, *Expendable Americans,* p. 13.
80. Brodeur, *Expendable Americans,* p. 146.
81. Solomon, "The Asbestos Fallout," p. 197.
82. For a discussion of specific deterrence, see Jack Gibbs, *Crime, Punishment, and Deterrence* (New York: Elsevier, 1975), pp. 34–35.
83. See ibid., pp. 38–39.
84. See *Asbestos-Related Occupational Diseases,* pp. 190–191, 203–211, 369.
85. Ibid., pp. 190–191; Solomon, "The Asbestos Fallout," p. 206.
86. *Asbestos Related Occupational Diseases,* p. 391.
87. Ibid., pp. 369 ff.
88. Ibid., Solomon, "The Asbestos Fallout," p. 206.

5

Deviance against customers

It is apparent that in regard to the federal antitrust laws, there has been a noticeable lack of large-scale, sustained, and well-publicized enforcement. In direct consequence, no large, visible group of convicted, stigmatized individuals has been created. This, in turn, has had profound effects upon various aspects of the societal reaction process directed against illegal corporate activities.

—*Albert E. McCormack, Jr.*[1]

83

The vulnerability of customers[2] and the protections they deserve are matters of debate. Some would protect customers from themselves by barring or at least discouraging sale of useless products. *Consumer Reports* and similar publications try to do this on a regular basis. Such efforts have not been broadly successful.

Protection of consumers from unsafe products has met with somewhat greater success. During the last twenty years the following corporations are among those forced to remedy defects or pay persons or their families injured or killed: General Motors for its Corvair,[3] Goodrich Tire and Rubber for its A7D airforce jet brake,[4] Beech Aircraft for its Beech Baron,[5] Ford Motor Company for its Pinto,[6] McDonnell Douglas for its DC–10,[7] and Richardson-Merrell for its drug MER/29.[8] However, it is impossible to determine how many safety problems have gone undetected or unpublicized.

Lastly, efforts to protect consumers from unfair prices by promoting and protecting competition among producers have met with limited success. The primary goal has been to maintain the number of competitors and prevent them from agreeing on prices among themselves. However, the number of competitors in many markets has continued to decline and meaningful price-fixing enforcement generally has been infrequent.[9] Customers often buy products where competition was expected to, but did not, determine prices.

Preview of the Chapter

Customers victimized by price-fixing are the subjects of this chapter. We first will examine the history of the Sherman Antitrust Act and the frequency of price-fixing. Then we will describe the electrical equipment price-fixing case. Lastly, we will analyze corporate deviance against publics-in-contact.

In describing the electrical equipment case, we will consider the mechanics of price-fixing and the precautions taken by participants to hide their actions from outsiders. We also will describe the discovery and prosecution of price-fixing and how executives and corporations defend their actions.

In analyzing this case, we will show how price-fixing grew out of the history of the industry. Then we will discuss market forces that provided incentives and rewards for price-fixing. Finally, we will discuss public attitudes towards price-fixing and the reasons for these attitudes.

THE SHERMAN ANTITRUST ACT

In the late 1800s, large nationwide corporations were gaining attention, but generally they were not an important public issue. Most businesses were small and locally owned and operated. There were few truly national corporations.

There were, however, two important exceptions. The railroad industry already was quite large, and a still growing nation had become dependent on the quick and generally efficient transportation it provided.[10] So, too, with the newly created Standard Oil trust.[11] Oil was becoming increasingly important, and, as in the case of the railroad industry, pricing behaviors in the oil industry were creating great concern.

Legislative response was quick and showed surprising consensus. In 1890 the Sherman Antitrust Act outlawed agreements among sellers on the prices charged customers. The Sherman Act passed the United States Senate unanimously and the House of Representatives with only one dissenting vote.

The Sherman Act was an attempt to preserve and encourage competitive markets by making price-fixing illegal.[12] A competitive market has many sellers competing for customers. Price-fixing agreements eliminate price-competition and discourage competition over quality. Additionally, price agreements can discourage new sellers as when established firms selectively charge artificially low prices to force less established firms to leave a market.

Price-fixing continues to be illegal, and recent congressional actions suggest some commitment to the maintenance of competitive markets. When the Sherman Act was first passed, violation of its price-fixing provisions was a misdemeanor punishable by a maximum of one year in prison. In 1974, Congress passed the "Antitrust Procedures and Penalty Act," which made price-fixing a felony punishable by a maximum of three years in prison.[13]

Frequency of Price-Fixing

The available evidence indicates that price-fixing is frequent. As part of his pioneering analysis of white-collar crime in 1949, Edwin Sutherland reported that forty-four of the seventy large corporations he studied had received 125 adverse price-fixing judgments.[14] Obviously, repeated violation was frequent, with 60 percent of convicted corporations being recidivists. Professor Sutherland further reported:

> The practice of price-fixing . . . is much more general than these decisions indicate. Charles M. Schwab, when asked whether the steel industry had agreements as to prices before the organization of the U.S. Steel Corporation, replied: "Yes, in all lines of business, not only in steel, but in everything else. They have existed in all lines of business as long as I can remember."[15]

The number of cases of antitrust violation alleged by the Department of Justice has remained high since Sutherland's era. There were 319 such cases in the 1940s, 294 in the 1950s, and 318 in the 1960s. The typical alleged violation was organized through a trade association or its equivalent, averaged fifteen or twenty firms, lasted six to ten years, and involved annual sales of $50 million to $150 million.[16]

More recently, Marshall B. Clinard studied the criminal actions of the nation's largest corporations during 1975 and 1976. Insofar as price-fixing is concerned, Professor Clinard reported:

> It is clear thar violations of the nation's antitrust laws are common . . . in a wide variety of industries. . . . Corporate executives themselves indicate that price-fixing is widespread.[17]

THE ELECTRICAL EQUIPMENT PRICE-FIXING CASE[18]

The electrical equipment industry sells equipment that generates, transmits, and controls electric power. In 1960, General Electric, Westinghouse, and twenty-seven other companies producing this equipment were caught in a massive price-fixing conspiracy that received more attention than such activities usually do. It was the subject of extended congressional hearings, three full books and chapters in others, numerous articles in professional and trade journals, and some newspaper articles and editorials.

In part, this attention reflected the sheer size of the case. This was a $1.75 billion dollar industry, and the defendants included twenty-nine different corporations and forty-five individuals. The companies paid almost $2 million in fines and ultimately paid many more millions in triple damage to their corporate victims. Also drawing attention was the fact that seven defendants, four of them vice-presidents of their companies and all respected in their communities, served twenty-five-day jail sentences. The case is noteworthy for what it tells us about the *mechanics* and *discovery* of price-fixing as well as how those involved mount a *defense* for their actions.

The Mechanics of Price-Fixing

This was not a case of companies accidentally or unknowingly stepping over a vague line between legal and illegal behavior. There could be no doubt that price-fixing is illegal:

> One interpretation [of the antitrust laws] has remained steady and un-swerving. That is the interpretation dealing with collusive agreements designed to fix prices, control production, and/or share markets. The courts have steadfastly maintained that collusive agreements which tamper with the free play of economic forces are *per se* violations of the Sherman Act. Once it has been proven that there was manipulation of prices, production, or market share, that is no [legal] defense open to the violators, such as a plea of reasonableness or no harm to competitors.[19]

There also can be little doubt that corporate executives who were involved knew their actions were illegal. They appear to have been well aware of the Sherman Antitrust Act, and they took numerous precautions to remain undetected. Each of them used some of the following techniques:

1. Phone calls were minimized.
2. When calls were made, public pay phones were used.
3. Except under unusual circumstances, no calls were made to the participants' offices.
4. Written communications were in plain envelopes mailed to participants' homes.
5. Written communications were supposed to be destroyed upon receipt.
6. Clandestine meetings were held at hunting lodges and hotels, never in corporate offices.
7. In going to meetings, participants were instructed not to travel on the same plane or train.
8. While at meetings, they did not use company names when registering.
9. While at meetings, they did not acknowledge one another's presence in restaurants or other public places.
10. No papers were left in private rooms following meetings.
11. Upon returning to their offices, participants filed false travel reports to mask their true destinations.
12. Communications used a series of code numbers to identify corporations.
13. Elaborate prearranged systems known as "phases of the moon" were sometimes used to fix prices automatically.

What they were hiding was an agreement to make a "reasonable" division of sales in order to preserve the existing market structure. Essentially, when bids came in, the company whose turn had come was allowed to submit its bid while the other participating companies submitted higher bids. In this way, the conspiracy maintained the existing market structure and eliminated price competition.

The obvious illegality of this scheme and the precautions taken to keep it secret might make observers think it was a conscious and continual source of concern for the participants. It was not. Most executives learned of the agreements when they first came to their jobs. They were informed that they were expected to fix prices as part of their work. Superiors took new recruits to their first meetings, introduced them to the "competition," and taught them how to hide their actions. Newcomers quickly took these activities in stride and no longer thought about them, save for the necessary precautions. Price-fixing became standard operating procedure, even for those whose personal beliefs and training at first made them reluctant participants. Most saw themselves as having a job to do. Price-fixing was part of that job, so they fixed prices.

Corporate Policy

Official policies of the companies, however, contained strongly worded statements emphasizing that price-fixing was illegal and contrary to company policy. Frequently, these policies were models of clarity and directness. From a distance they suggest that no right-thinking executive would even consider price-fixing, much less engage in it. At General Electric, for instance, a carefully written preamble cautioning against price-fixing was followed by this antiprice-fixing policy statement:

> It is the Policy of the Company to comply strictly in all respects with the antitrust laws. There shall be no exception to this Policy, nor shall it be compromised or qualified by anyone acting for or on behalf of the Company. No employee shall enter into any understanding, agreement, plan or scheme, expressed or implied, formal or informal, with any competitor, in regard to prices, terms, or conditions of sale, production, distribution, territories or customers; nor exchange or discuss with a competitor prices, terms or conditions of sale or any other competitive information; nor engage in any other conduct which in the opinion of the company's counsel, violates any of the antitrust laws ... [I]f an employee is convicted of violating the law, the Company cannot as a matter of law save the employee from whatever punishment the court may impose on him as a consequence of such conviction.[20]

There were regular exhortations to comply with this policy and equally regular requirements that compliance be certified in writing. But the many people involved in price-fixing discounted these, either because exhortations always seemed to occur during lulls when no price-fixing was occurring anyway or because they were seen as reflecting a peculiar commitment to competition by certain executives. Participants, therefore, kept knowledge of price-fixing away from some executives and from company lawyers. Even when the conspiracy was first collapsing, executives lied to their corporate superiors and attorneys.

Nonetheless, top corporate executives not involved directly should have known, and probably did know, that price-fixing was occurring and had been occurring for a very long time. Some of them had engaged in it earlier in their own careers, only to oppose it publicly when promoted. Understandably, their conversions did not seem to carry great conviction to those below them. Price-fixing continued as a way of life.

The Discovery of Price-Fixing

In this case, discovery of price-fixing was not easy. First, there were the already described precautions intended to keep communications and meetings secret. Second, there was the large number of separate agreements. Price-fixing was not the result of a single conspiracy. Instead, it was a set of twenty somewhat independent agreements on products ranging from two-dollar insulators to million-dollar turbines. Some involved as few as three firms whereas the largest had eight. Most firms produced only a few of the products and, therefore, participated in only a few of the agreements. Thus, discovery of one conspiracy did not necessarily lead to the discovery of others.

Third, the agreements were not continuous. A company or product line might withdraw from price-fixing for a few years despite pressures from colleagues wishing to present a united front. It would usually return when the economy turned sour and prices became half or less of what they were when price-fixing rather than markets determined prices.

Finally, discovery was difficult because the corporations involved in these shifting networks were remarkably diverse. They ranged from industry giants such as General Electric and Westinghouse to Joselyn Manufacturing, a small company involved in only four conspiracies. Joselyn's total manufacturing space was about the size of the courtroom in which it later was tried for price-fixing.

The people involved were equally diverse:

> There was J. E. Cordell, ex-submariner, sales vice-president of Southern
> States Equipment Corporation, pillar of the community in a small Georgia
> town, though his net worth never exceeded $25,000, and urbane William
> S. Ginn, G.E. vice-president at $135,000 a year, a man once thought to be
> on his way to the presidency of the corporation. There were old, portly
> Fred F. Loock, president of Allen-Bradley Company, who found conspiring
> with competitors quite to his taste ("It is the only way a business can run;
> it is free enterprise"), and Marc A. deFerranti, who pocketed his repug-
> nance on orders from his boss. There was M. H. Howard, a production
> manager of Foster Wheeler, who found it hard to stay in the conspiracy
> (his company's condenser business ran in the red during two years of it),
> and C. H. Wheeler Manufacturing's President Thomas, who found it hard
> to quit—he'd been told his firm couldn't survive if he left the cartel.[21]

Discovery of these multiple and shifting arrangements involving
diverse products, corporations, and executives was not easy. No single
confession or piece of evidence uncovered them. Rather, it was a complicated process involving a great deal of prosecutorial persistence and
luck. Many attempts were made to gather information, and some succeeded. In the end, four different grand juries and testimony of 196
persons were required to uncover all of the conspiracies.

What was unusual was that, at the end of the process, information
emerged of much greater quality than normally exists. Through good
fortune and diligence, the Justice Department uncovered a set of richly
detailed documents. As the attorney general at the time said: "I was
amazed. I did not believe what I saw. Before me were not the usual
vague, general statements usually encountered in antitrust cases, but
specific facts, all accusing the electrical equipment industry of things
which were as vast as anything yet realized in the entire history of the
Sherman Act."[22] His surprise and joy are more understandable when
we consider that grand juries had investigated price-fixing in this industry before, but none had succeeded.

The Investigative Process

Information was gathered initially to force out additional disclosures
that, in turn, created still more information. Among the events in this
process that led to indictments were the following:

1. The Tennessee Valley Authority (TVA) long had complained about
   receiving identical "secret" bids, and about American prices that were
   too high. For instance, two years before the price-fixing was exposed,
   TVA faced rapidly rising prices and decided to buy overseas. Prices

there were two-thirds of the U.S. price and could not be explained away by lower labor costs or similar relative advantages. TVA also complained about receiving absolutely identical bids a year later on everything from three-dollar insulators to seventeen-million-dollar generators. These complaints increasingly were made in public and found their way to the press.

2. Senator Kefauver of Tennessee chaired a powerful Senate committee and read of the TVA complaints in a home state newspaper. His subsequent threat to hold investigative hearings is said to have prodded the Department of Justice to initiate its own investigation.[23]

3. As is typical in such cases, grand juries began by subpoenaing documents. With these documents in hand, they began to subpoena individuals. First were the least important companies and lowest-level personnel. As the amount of information grew, grand juries gradually enlarged their scope and increased the rank and size of personnel and corporations.

4. An employee of Lapp Insulator Company became scared and told a grand jury all he knew about one of the conspiracies. His decision set off a chain of events within G.E. where people confessed to company lawyers of their involvement in this and some other schemes. Lapp was only involved in two agreements, however, so its information was limited.

5. There were strong divisions among the defendants. Preferential treatment of one important General Electric executive, as well as the ultimate firing of others, cut defendant loyalty to the company and sent many executives running to government prosecutors. Similarly, as cases proliferated and new grand juries were formed, a momentum built and attorneys frequently sought client immunity. "[L]awyers began popping up trying to get immunity for their clients in return for testimony. Scarcely a week went by that [the chief prosecutor] didn't get information on at least two new cases."[24]

6. In one important case, a government attorney visited an old college classmate who had become president of a small manufacturing company. The visitor had the express goal of learning what his friend knew about the price-fixing. The visit produced enough so that the Justice Department could frighten one of the larger companies, I.T.E., whose lawyers did an internal check.

   What they found was startling. One young I.T.E. manager had violated agreed-upon procedures. He had not destroyed his records. This violation resulted not from perversity or honesty, but rather because he had the role of secretary. He wanted records in order to fulfill his secretarial responsibilities and to be able to train his successor.

   The damning records thus were a product of the normal need for record-keeping. There was a conflict between conspiratorial need to destroy evidence and the bureaucratic need to keep records. In this case, the latter won. These records were crucial to the investigation.

7. The availability of I.T.E. records, in turn, frightened the Allis-Chalmers Corporation, which was then third in the electrical equipment industry with sales of about $500 million dollars. Allis-Chalmers decided to make a deal. If the government would go easy on the corporation, the corporation would cooperate by providing "solid" information. The corporation fulfilled its part of the bargain, submitting thousands cf documents useful in the case. These materials exposed new cases that had not yet been uncovered.

    In the end the Allis-Chalmers decision gave prosecutors one further advantage. Allis-Chalmers had agreed to plead guilty in those cases where it was involved, eight in all. With this company pleading guilty, it would have been far more difficult for its co-conspirators to maintain their claim of innocence.

8. The presiding judge prohibited "no contest" pleas unless agreed to by the government, although judges typically permitted this plea in similar cases.

    A no contest plea would not have required defendants to admit their guilt. Nor would they have had to maintain that they were innocent.

    Because they would not have pleaded innocent, there would have been no need for a trial. But because they would not have admitted guilt, plaintiffs in subsequent civil suits still would have had to prove guilt.

    A no contest plea thus would have produced a quiet proceeding in which the corporations were fined slightly, but their guilt was not put on the record nor their documents made public. The judge in the electrical cases prohibited no contest pleas unless the government agreed. For more serious cases the government would not agree, so information became public and guilt assigned.[25]

In sum, discovery of the conspiracies was slow, complex, and fortuitous. It produced a remarkably detailed description of the mechanics and discovery of price-fixing. It also permits analysis of the ways in which executives and corporations defend involvement in price-fixing.

Defending Price-Fixing

The corporations and executives involved in these cases did not sit by idly and allow themselves to be labeled deviant. They instead used their power to attempt to defend or "account"[26] for their actions. These accounts were variable and occasionally innovative.

The largest of the defendants, General Electric, was involved in nineteen of the twenty conspiracies. It tried to separate the actions of individuals from those of the corporation. G.E. treated admissions of price-fixing as admissions by individuals that they had violated corporate policy. In support of this stand, the company elite emphasized that executives in the very top leadership of the company did not know what was going on and that those below had acted beyond authority given by the company. They further emphasized that company policy against price-fixing was both strong and clear. They argued that price-fixing, therefore, had not been a corporate act, but rather the action of wayward individuals whom the corporation would punish.

It is important to note that G.E.'s stance struck many observers at the time, including the trial judge, as scapegoating. Observers argued that middle-level managers were responding to real but unwritten corporate policies and pressures. They also pointed to evidence indicating that top executives almost certainly were aware of, and had condoned, price-fixing activities of subordinates. The trial judge, for instance, observed:

> One would be most naive indeed to believe that these violations of the law, so long persisted in, affecting so large a segment of the industry and finally involving so many millions of dollars were facts unknown to those responsible for the corporation and its conduct. . . .[27]

Accusations of scapegoating notwithstanding, it is clear that G.E. advanced a traditional defense of its corporate deviance. G.E. accounted for its deviance by claiming that "bad apples"[28] in the otherwise clean barrel were responsible for price-fixing. Overzealous and possibly immoral people fixed prices; G.E. did not.

Westinghouse also was involved in nineteen conspiracies, but it could not be accused of scapegoating. Its corporate elite publicly defined the price-fixing as a sign of organization problems rather than an indicator of individual failures. In defending this stance, spokespersons argued that middle-level corporate managers who had engaged in price-fixing were reputable people, had not transgressed for personal gain, had suffered enough, and were unlikely to repeat their errors. They were claiming in essence that their people were not "true" criminals, but were basically honest people who had made one slip not in keeping with their character.

It is important to note that the Westinghouse stance also had its problems. It ignored the individual gains and rewards for price-fixing. Individuals who cooperated were rewarded with promotions and salary increases. Westinghouse's position also ignored the obvious fact that defendants in all criminal cases suffer. Electrical executives hardly were unique in this respect. Similarly, the reputability of those involved was not a result of never having fixed prices before. They had. It instead was a result of never having been caught.

Whereas G.E. blamed its employees and Westinghouse blamed itself, the remaining smaller corporations advanced a variety of novel defenses. Each smaller company accounted for its involvement in one or more of the following ways:

1. The company was small and hence not important in the case. ("We were involved, but ours was an unimportant contribution.")
2. The company made no profit from its activity. ("We were involved, but we did not make any money from it.")
3. The company had only followed the leaders and had no choice. ("We were involved, but we were forced to fix prices by the larger corporations.")
4. The company's previous record in antitrust cases had been good. ("We were involved, but we hadn't previously been convicted for fixing prices.")
5. The company had not been involved in the conspiracy as long as others. ("We were involved, but not for very long.")
6. The company was being subjected to double jeopardy in the form of criminal and civil trials. ("We were involved, but it's not fair to punish us twice.")
7. The triple-damage civil suits that guilty pleas might bring would ruin the company. ("We were involved, but it's not fair or wise possibly to destroy the company.")
8. The Justice Department was being unfairly harsh. ("We were involved, but they are picking on us.")

Individual defendants had an equally varied bag of defenses. At one time or another, defendants advanced the following explanations for their actions:

1. The defendant was not a criminal type and should not be thrown in jail with "common criminals who have been convicted of embezzlement and other serious crimes."[29] ("Some people are criminal throughout their character whereas other people, especially people like the defendants, are essentially noncriminal. Arsonists thus are not just criminal when setting fires, but also criminal in some general way in which we price-fixers are not.")
2. Price-fixing laws were vague. ("Although we took elaborate precautions to hide our actions, we did not know our actions were illegal.")
3. We were just following orders. ("Although some of our colleagues refused to fix prices and were not severely sanctioned for their refusal, we had no choice.")
4. We enjoyed no personal gains from price-fixing. ("We realized no immediate personal advantage for price-fixing although we did know that persons who had previously fixed prices had been promoted to positions of power and responsibility.")
5. Price-fixing is illegal by the letter of the law, but it is not immoral because the public really doesn't care about price-fixing. ("We were involved, but it was not an important transgression.")

The corporations and executives caught in price-fixing were thus quick to defend their actions. Central to nearly all of these defenses were attempts to explain to outsiders why prices are fixed. Also central were requests for leniency by reason of the circumstances surrounding involvement.

ANALYSIS OF DEVIANCE AGAINST CUSTOMERS

A person can too easily stand from afar and view this case of corporate deviance as a failure of individuals, of corporations, or both. After all, corporations are supposed to compete—when they do not, something is wrong. But this initial view must be tempered by John Kenneth Galbraith's observation about price-fixing's being "principally deplored by university professors on life-long appointments. Such security of tenure is deemed essential for fruitful and unremitting thought."[30] Just as professors have partially self-serving and partially valid beliefs, so too are the beliefs of electric companies' executives not created in a vacuum.

A review of attitudes toward competition shows that Americans have regularly advocated competition, particularly for others, but also have engaged in activities suggesting a healthy ability to cooperate and reduce competition. Until recently, airline ticket prices were not determined by competition, milk prices still are not, and producers in most industries get together to set many standards and even prices.

Keeping these cautionary observations in mind, we now will analyze the heavy electrical equipment case. We begin by considering the history of cooperation among manufacturers. Then we will discuss the importance of oligopolistic and volatile markets. Lastly, we will discuss reasons for current public attitudes toward price-fixing.

A History of Cooperation

Price-fixing did not emerge full grown, nor was it the result of a careful plan. Instead, its growth was fostered unintentionally by a history of cooperation among manufactuers, some of it encouraged by government.

Electrical industry cooperation traces back at least to the 1920s. In 1926 a trade association that had had its rudimentary beginnings in 1905 emerged as the National Electrical Manufacturers Association. One of its goals, in keeping with the "open prices" belief of the day, was to share price information. Such sharing was not publicly discouraged. In fact, in the words of a 1925 Supreme Court ruling, "competition does not become less free merely because the conduct of commercial operations becomes more intelligent through free distribution of knowledge of all the essential factors entering into the commercial transaction."[31] Exchange of pricing data thus was promoted by industry and by government, at least by its judicial branch.

Open pricing received additional support during the depression of the 1930s. Both industry and government at that time encouraged collaboration to stablize prices, which were falling dramatically. The electrical industry and its leader, General Electric, were deeply involved in this stabilization movement. In September of 1931, for example, the G.E. president made the front page of major newspapers with a speech entitled "Stabilization of Industry," which proposed "a new constitution for industry designed to stabilize production and consumption, to minimize unemployment and to solve adequately the problem of security for the worker and his family. . . ."[32] This would be done by trade associations with a multitude of goals, including "stabilization of prices." In the context of the great depression, such ideas had wide appeal.

Government support for price stabilization came in the form of the National Recovery Act (NRA). The NRA was passed in 1933 after strong endorsement from President Roosevelt, himself past president of a trade association. More than four-fifths of the first 677 NRA codes made provision for minimum prices. The NRA, however, was declared illegal in 1935, thus ending government efforts to keep prices from falling below agreed-upon minimums.

World War II brought government back into the business of setting prices; only this time its goal was to keep them from rising above established maximums. The Office of Price Administration (OPA) was established in 1941 to set price ceilings in an effort to contain war-related inflation.[33] These ceilings were established by government, but industry could lobby to raise them. Members of the electrical industry, therefore, cooperated in an entirely legal effort to increase their OPA ceilings. The story of one of the participants in both the early legal OPA and later illegal price-fixing meetings is typical:

Burke's introduction to the heavy-equipment conspiracy was easy as falling off a log. It occurred when he reported . . . as sales manager. [His supervisor] called the new man in and told him he'd be expected to attend a Pittsburgh meeting of the transformer section of the National Electrical Manufacturer's Association. . . . The talk . . . was about prices, OPA-regulated prices, and how the industry could best argue Washington into jacking up the ceilings. Burke didn't consider this illegal, and he took part in several subsequent meetings before OPA was abolished.[34]

For Mr. Burke and others, price meetings continued even after the OPA lapsed. However, they no longer responded to prices determined by government decree. Instead, the participants began to agree upon prices among themselves. Legal meetings to plan political lobbying had facilitated illegal meetings to fix prices.

In sum, manufacturers of electrical equipment had a history of legal cooperation. Much of this cooperation resulted from industry actions such as formation of the National Electrical Manufacturers Association. Government encouraged such cooperation, initially via supportive court rulings and later with agencies intended to control prices (NRA and OPA). A framework for cooperation of all types, including price-fixing, thus was created by the combined actions of business and government.

An Oligopolistic Market

Equally important in understanding the origins of price-fixing was the market structure that made it possible. Price-fixing was facilitated by a market that was highly concentrated (oligopolistic). Only a few firms sold in each of the submarkets of the electrical industry, so cooperation was relatively easy. By contrast, agriculture and the restaurant business have so many farms and restaurants that price-fixing networks would be impossible to initiate, organize, and maintain. Cooperation thus is enhanced when the number of participants is low.

Only one electrical conspiracy involved more than ten participants. In most pacts the participants enjoyed complete control of their submarket. With few exceptions, no firm selling of a product was outside the agreement, and, for those exceptions, at least three or four producers did participate. The oligopolistic electrical equipment market structure thus facilitated price-fixing.

A Volatile Market

Production of heavy electrical equipment requires extremely expensive equipment, which must be paid for whether or not it is being used. This machinery cannot be "laid off" when sales or profits decline. Research costs also are high and cannot be avoided for fear of falling behind the competition. Thus, many costs are fixed at a high level regardless of the level of sales. If sales decline, costs nonetheless remain high and the firms take a financial beating.

Unfortunately, this is exactly what frequently happened. There were, of course, the normal variations in sales that occur in most industries. In addition, customers for electrical equipment had surplus capacity, so they sometimes could wait a year or two until prices came down. While they waited, sales declined precipitously, and profits turned to losses.

As a result of high fixed costs combined with changing levels of sales income, the industry was highly volatile. Profits and sales went up and down dramatically. Lean periods were followed by affluent periods and shortly again by lean periods. In the decade following World War I, for instance, electrical industry sales tripled, only to decline back below their previous level in the following ten years. Price collusion attempted to dampen this otherwise uncontrollable and unpredictable situation.

Price-fixing in this and many other cases[35] thus was defensive. It was not used to maximize profits. Rather, it was a mechanism to minimize fluctuations and losses. It tended to exist when prices and sales were low and to be suspended when market situations became better. Of course, it also was suspended when law enforcement agencies momentarily made risks outweigh benefits:

> When the market behaved in a manner the executives thought satisfactory, or when enforcement agencies seemed particularly threatening, the conspiracy desisted. When market conditions deteriorated, while corporate pressures for achieving attractive profit-and-loss statements remained constant, and enforcement activity abated, the price-fixing agreements flourished.[36]

Lack of Public Concern

Most people do not attach great importance to social norms prohibiting price-fixing. This is because they rarely hear about price-fixing, because the cost of any single product is not that important to them, because the harm is not physical, and because corporations effectively offer counterdefinitions of their behavior.

Most people rarely hear about price-fixing because corporate executives involved in it take successful precautions to hide their actions from outsiders. Discovery, therefore, is a painstaking and infrequent process. And, even when price-fixing is discovered, newspapers devote little attention to it.

People are not greatly concerned about extra costs caused by the few publicized instances of price-fixing. They produce some goods and services while simultaneously being customers for others. However, they are most concerned when protecting their interests as producers. This is rational because they individually produce a limited range of outputs, the continued production of which is crucial to their well-being. But they are consumers of a wide range of goods and services, no one of which is nearly as important to them.

Thus, the price and costs of electrical equipment are crucially important for the selling companies and the individuals employed by them. However, for publics-in-contact with these organizations, the contact is one small part of their total activities. Even purchasers of electrical equipment do so as one of many activities. They understandably direct only a small amount of their emotion to this activity.

People also are not greatly concerned with price-fixing because the harm it produces is financial, not physical. The consequences of price-fixing are not as clear or physical as those that result from corporate dumping of toxic substances at Love Canal or from the exposing of employees to asbestos dust by Johns-Manville. As a recent survey suggests, "direct and physical impact are key criteria in the public's assessment of the seriousness of organizational offences."[37]

Finally, the public is unconcerned because those accused of price-fixing are able to offer effective defenses for their behaviors. Corporations have resources, such as ready access to the media, to promote vigorously counterdefinitions of their activities.[38] They use these resources to prevent negative definitions from gaining widespread attention and to promote their own more favorable definitions of their activities.

Corporations enjoy numerous options in this regard. A corporation can acknowledge a deviant act and promise that it will not recur, pointing to internal measures intended to prevent a recurrence—the approach adopted by Westinghouse. It can reject as untrue the definition of itself or its acts as deviant, as General Electric did when it placed blame on wayward employees. A corporation also can offer accounts to justify or excuse its behaviors. These explanations frequently are available because most social events are open to a variety of interpretations. Corporations and individual executives can, therefore, select explanations that strike responsive chords in a society, the range of which was shown earlier in this chapter.

For these reasons and likely others,[39] most people are not much concerned about price-fixing. Price-fixing remains illegal, but weak public attitudes and enforcement make it only marginally deviant.

It, therefore, is unrealistic to expect businesspeople and their corporations to abhor or refrain from actions most outsiders really don't care about very much.[40] In saying this, we recognize that corporations encourage the lack of public concern. And we also recognize that perhaps it would be possible to generate public alarm about price-fixing. But, as matters currently stand, there is little to stop corporations from fixing prices. And so, corporations understandably continue to fix prices, and most people continue not to care.

SUMMARY

Fierce and untrammeled competition is advocated in corporate stockholder meetings, political debate, and some economic classes and on other ceremonial occasions. But competition often is more trammeled than rhetoric and ceremony might suggest, sometimes for good reason. Trade associations and some governmental actions can encourage price agreements, as can unpredictable and oligopolistic markets and unconcerned publics. For many reasons, however, these acts meet with only moderate disapproval.

ANNOTATED SELECTED READINGS

Anthony, William, and Joel Haynes. "Consumerism: A Three Generation Paradigm." *University of Michigan Business Review* 26 (November 1975):21–26. Describes three stages in attitudes toward consumer rights since the late 1800s.

Clinard, Marshall B. *The Black Market: A Study of White Collar Crime.* New York: Rinehart and Company, 1952. An in-depth, morally outraged study of the World War II black market in meat, gasoline, and housing. Looks at the extent of the black market, methods of control, and public responses to price controls.

Heilbroner, Robert L., et al., eds. *In the Name of Profit.* New York: Warner Paperback Library, 1973. A series of six well-written exposés of the things companies do for profit, including sale of drugs, automobiles, and napalm.

Lane, Robert E. "Why Businessmen Violate the Law." *The Journal of Criminal Law, Criminology and Police Science* 44 (1953):151–165. Concludes that violations of labor and trade laws were related to social pressures and personal experiences of businessmen and also to organizational financial difficulty.

Miller, Arthur R. *The Assault on Privacy.* New York: Signet Books, 1972. Discussion of legal, technical, and governmental issues regarding personal privacy.

Smith, Richard Austin. "The Incredible Electrical Conspiracy." Reprinted in Richard Austin Smith, *Corporations in Crises.* New York: Anchor/Doubleday, 1966. Pp. 113–166. Thorough description and analysis of the electrical price-fixing cases, originally published in *Fortune.*

Vandivier, Kermit. "Why Should My Conscience Bother Me?" Reprinted in M. David Ermann and Richard Lundman, eds., *Corporate and Governmental Deviance.* New York: Oxford U.P., 1978. Insider's personal story of Goodrich's designing of inadequate brakes to be used on military aircraft.

Walton, Clarence C., and Frederick W. Cleveland, Jr. *Corporations on Trial: The Electric Cases.* Belmont, CA: Wadsworth, 1964. A history and analysis of the electrical conspiracy.

NOTES

1. Albert E. McCormack, Jr., "Rule Enforcement and Moral Indignation: Some Observations on the Effects of Criminal Antitrust Convictions upon Societal Reaction Processes," *Social Problems* 25 (October 1977): 35.
2. Customers are the most common publics-in-contact with corporations, but not the only ones. Others include those who sell to, receive charity from, and have credit ratings compiled by corporations. For a discussion of publics-in-contact with business and other organizations, see Peter M. Blau and W. Richard Scott, *Formal Organizations* (San Francisco: Chandler Publishing, 1962), pp. 44–55.
3. Ralph Nader, *Unsafe at Any Speed* (New York: Grossman Publishers, 1965).
4. Kermit Vandivier, "Why Should My Conscience Bother Me?" in M. David Ermann and Richard J. Lundman, eds., *Corporate and Governmental Deviance* (New York: Oxford U.P., 1978), pp. 80–101.
5. Moria Johnston, *The Last Nine Minutes: The Story of Flight 981* (New York: Avon, 1978), pp. 208–221.
6. Mark Dowie, "Pinto Madness," *Mother Jones* II(September/October 1977): 18–24.
7. Johnston, *The Last Nine Minutes;* Paul Eddy, Elaine Potter, and Bruce Page, *Destination Disaster: From the Tri-Motor to the DC–10* (New York: The New York Times Book Company, 1976).
8. Sanford J. Ungar, "Get Away with What You Can," in Robert L. Heilbroner et al., *In the Name of Profit* (Garden City, NY: Doubleday, 1972), 106–127.
9. See McCormack, "Rule Enforcement."
10. See Sanford D. Gordon, "Attitudes Towards Trusts Prior to the Sherman Act," *Southern Economics Journal* 30 (October 1963): 156–167.
11. John Neil Story and Lynn M. Ward, *Perspectives of American Law: Cases on Law and Society* (St. Paul, MN: West Publishing Company, 1974), p. 389. See also Gordon, "Attitudes."
12. See Story and Ward, *Perspectives,* pp. 379–388; Lee Fusilier and Jerome C. Darnell, *Competition and Public Policy: Cases in Antitrust* (Englewood

Cliffs, NJ: Prentice-Hall, 1971). John Kenneth Galbraith has argued that antitrust laws are an "anachronism." See *The New Industrial State* (Boston: Houghton Mifflin, 1967), p. 206.

13. Jeffrey H. Reiman, *The Rich Get Richer and the Poor Get Prison: Ideology, Class, and Criminal Justice* (New York: Wiley, 1979), p. 136.
14. Edwin H. Sutherland, *White-Collar Crime* (New York: Holt, Rinehart and Winston, 1949), pp. 58–69.
15. Ibid., p. 88.
16. Richard Posner, "A Statistical Study of Antitrust Enforcement." *The Journal of Law and Economics* 13 (October 1970): 365–419.
17. Marshall B. Clinard, *Illegal Corporate Behavior* (Washington, DC: U.S. Government Printing Office, 1979), p. 184.
18. This section is based primarily on the following sources: Clarence C. Walton and Frederick W. Cleveland, Jr., *Corporations on Trial: The Electric Cases* (Belmont, CA: Wadsworth, 1964); John Herling, *The Great Price Conspiracy* (Washington, DC: Luce, 1962); John G. Fuller, *The Gentleman Conspirators* (New York: Grove, 1962); Gilbert Geis, "White-Collar Crime: The Heavy Electrical Equipment Antitrust Cases of 1961," in M. David Ermann and Richard J. Lundman, eds., *Corporate and Governmental Deviance* (New York: Oxford U.P., 1978), pp. 59–79; Senate Committee on the Judiciary, Subcommittee on Antitrust and Monopoly, 87th Congress 2nd Session, 1961, "Administered Prices," *Hearings,* PTS 27 and 28; Richard Austin Smith, "The Incredible Electrical Conspiracy," reprinted in Richard Austin Smith, *Corporations in Crisis* (New York: Anchor/Doubleday, 1966), pp. 113–166.
19. Fusilier and Darnell, *Competition,* p. 199.
20. Walton and Cleveland, *Corporations,* p. 67.
21. Smith, "The Incredible," p. 114.
22. Walton and Cleveland, *Corporations,* p. 34.
23. According to one observer, 95 percent of Department of Justice antitrust activities are initiated in response to complaints. This case is thus typical. See Mark J. Green, *The Closed Enterprise System* (New York: Grossman Publishers, 1972), p. 78.
24. Smith, "The Incredible," pp. 148–149.
25. There are many analogies to the uncovering of the Watergate conspiracy. One employee (John Dean) came forward with a great deal of information, congressional hearings prompted Department of Justice action, dramatic documentary information was brought forward with the surprising disclosure of the taping system, various individual defendants began to scurry for cover and make deals with prosecutors, a judge was tough, and prosecutors were lucky.
26. See William B. Waegel, M. David Ermann, and Alan M. Horowitz, "Organizational Responses to Imputations of Deviance," *The Sociological Quarterly* (forthcoming, 1981).
27. Smith, "The Incredible," p. 115.

28. Police administrators routinely blame "bad apples" for police misconduct. For a discussion of this, see Lawrence W. Sherman, ed., *Police Corruption: A Sociological Perspective* (Garden City, NY: Anchor Books, 1974), pp. 7–8.

29. Geis, "White-Collar," p. 59.

30. John Kenneth Galbraith, *Economics & The Public Purpose* (Boston: Houghton Mifflin, 1973), p. 56.

31. Walton and Cleveland, *Corporations,* p. 5.

32. Ibid., p. 7.

33. See Marshall B. Clinard, *The Black Market: A Study of White-Collar Crime* (New York: Rinehart and Company, 1952).

34. Smith, "The Incredible," p. 121.

35. For example, see Jeffrey Sonnenfeld and Paul R. Lawrence, "Why Do Companies Succumb to Price Fixing?" *Harvard Business Review* (July–August 1979): 147–148.

36. Geis, "White-Collar Crime," pp. 78–79.

37. Laura Shill Schrager and James P. Short, Jr., "Toward a Sociology of Organizational Crime," *Social Problems* 25 (1978): 408.

38. See Waegel et al., "Organizational Responses"; M. David Ermann, "The Operative Goals of Corporate Philanthropy," *Social Problems* 25 (June 1978): 504–514.

39. McCormack, "Rule Enforcement," argues that lack of enforcement produces weak public attitudes toward violations of antitrust laws.

40. See Sanford H. Kadish, "Some Observations on the Use of Criminal Sanctions in Enforcing Economic Regulations, in Gilbert Geis and Robert F. Meier, eds., *White-Collar Crime: Offenses in Business, Politics and the Professions,* rev. ed. (New York: Free Press, 1977), pp. 306–315.

Deviance against the public-at-large

As James Madison recognized nearly 200 years ago in *Federalist No. 10,* the efforts of economic interests to influence government have been a staple of American politics. Electoral involvement . . . by corporations around the turn of the century . . . evoked, not surprisingly, a strong reaction among those elements of American society which felt themselves to be severely disadvantaged politically by the ability of these organizations to bring to the electoral arena levels of financial and organizational resources not available to ordinary citizens.

—Edwin M. Epstein [1]

Corporations can use their resources to influence the political process in many ways. In elections, they can contribute services ranging from typewriters to office space to company airplanes to employees on leave but still paid by the firm. They can use their resources to encourage employees, stockholders, or customers to make political contributions, or they can contribute directly from corporate funds or indirectly by issuing employee bonuses with the understanding that these will be contributed to particular candidates. They can pay a candidate's firm for nonexistent or overpriced legal or other services or pay the candidate handsomely for speaking to corporate dealers or executives. They can buy expensive advertisements in party convention books or expensive meals at candidates' fundraisers. And they can sponsor television programs, documentaries, news stories, or press releases.[2]

Currently, most such activities are prohibited by law and periodically disapproved by the public-at-large. Federal law makes it illegal for business corporations to make financial contributions to candidates for national office. Many states have similar laws making it illegal for corporations to contribute to candidates for state office. The rationale for such laws is a perception that individuals and corporations differ in their abilities to aid candidates for public office. Obvious differences in financial resources give corporations obvious advantages in influencing candidates. The law tries to protect the public-at-large by forbidding corporate political contributions.

Preview of the Chapter

The purpose of this chapter is to describe and analyze corporate deviance against the public-at-large. Our specific focus is on corporate violations of Corrupt Practices Acts. We begin by describing the origins of such acts and the nature of their enforcement following Watergate. We then will describe and analyze the acts of one corporate violator, Gulf Oil.

Our description of these acts will show the elaborate precautions organized elites take to hide their actions. In the case of Gulf Oil, these precautions included money laundering and secret distribution systems impervious to discovery for at least twelve years.

Our analyses will direct attention to organizational characteristics and environments. We will examine Gulf as an organization, emphasizing rationalizations, corporate roles, and employee loyalty. We then will combine analysis of Gulf with material from earlier chapters to form a model of how corporate deviance frequently proceeds. Finally, we will discuss the importance of external corporate environments, emphasizing the complementary interests of big government and big business.

CORRUPT PRACTICES ACTS[3]

Prior to 1907, corporate campaign contributions were both legal and frequent. The privately owned United States Bank, for instance, spent $80,000 just for pamphleteering in the 1832 presidential campaign. Sugar refiners spent large sums in 1892 in an effort to dictate sugar tariffs. And Standard Oil, one of the first truly national corporations, spent $500,000 in the 1896 and 1900 elections.

Corporations making campaign contributions generally were those most directly dependent on government regulations and decisions. For example, between 1888 and 1900, politicians were attempting to decide where to locate a canal linking the Atlantic and Pacific Oceans. Corporations interested in building the canal variously lobbied that it should be located through Nicaragua or across the Isthmus of Panama. Here is part of what happened:

> The elder Senator La Follette tells us that preceding the presidential election of 1888 Republican leaders urged him to support the Nicaraguan Canal Bill because parties interested in its passage had offered to contribute $100,000 to the Republican campaign fund if the bill were acted upon favorably. A similar amount had been offered to the Democrats.[4]

A small number of people had been concerned about such contributions since the late 1800s. However, corporate campaign contributions only started to become an important public issue in the United States in the final weeks of the 1904 presidential election. The Democratic candidate, Judge Alton B. Parker, charged that his Republican opponent, Teddy Roosevelt, had accepted large contributions from conservatives wanting government favors.

Judge Parker and other Democratic campaigners refused to accept corporate contributions and linked Republican support for high tariffs to corporate contributions. On October 24, 1904, Judge Parker asked:

> Shall the creations of government, many of which pursue illegal methods, control our elections, control them by moneys belonging to their stockholders, moneys not given in the open and charged upon the books as moneys paid for political purposes, but hidden by false bookkeeping?[5]

Republicans did not directly respond to Judge Parker's charges, the issue having been raised very late in the campaign. They instead noted that both parties had been in the habit of receiving corporate contributions, denied they had made any promises in return for contributions, and claimed that Democrats also were accepting corporate money.

The issue did not play a major role in the election because public opinion "had not been sufficiently aroused to declare itself."[6] The issue was strong enough, however, outlive the election and help foster significant changes in the sources and disclosure of political contributions. In his message to Congress in December of 1905, President Roosevelt recommended a law abolishing corporate political contributions. And, in January of 1907, Congress passed such a bill.

Similar laws were passed at the state level. There already were five state laws prohibiting corporate political contributions by 1905, twenty-one by 1910, and thirty-five by 1920.[7] These laws, along with their federal counterparts, came to be called "corrupt practices acts" and dealt with many aspects of campaign financing. They reflected a general public concern about rampant political corruption.

Corporate contributions were seen as one part of this larger problem of corruption. But corporate contributions are quite different from ordinary small bribes for specific favors because they usually have more general and less identifiable goals. Hence, the reasons for their criminalization were not clear to the public or even to some judges.[8]

Perhaps because of the lack of clarity, enforcement efforts directed at corporations essentially have been nonexistent. Corporate contributions have been described as a part of corporate and political life,[9] but contributors and recipients of these illegal funds have not been quick to reveal their illegal transactions. Additionally, enforcement officials have not devoted resources to the discovery and prosecution of corporate offenders. As a consequence, these laws rarely had been enforced. Watergate changed that.

Enforcement Following The Watergate Break-in

On June 17, 1972 a private security guard found evidence of a break-in at the Watergate complex in Washington. Police were called, and five men were arrested inside the Democratic National Committee Headquarters. The five were well-funded and well-equipped and generally were not ordinary burglars. They had been

dressed in business suits and all had worn Playtex rubber surgical gloves. Police . . . seized a walkie-talkie, 40 rolls of unexposed film, two 35-millimeter cameras, lock picks, pen-size tear-gas guns, and bugging devices . . . apparently . . . capable of picking up both telephone and room conversations.[10]

Part of the ensuing investigation focused on identifying the sources of funding for the Watergate break-in and other illegal Nixon administration actions. In July of 1973, Watergate Special Prosecutor Archibald Cox announced that his office had evidence that American Airlines had made an illegal $55,000 corporate contribution to the Committee to Re-Elect the President (CREEP).[11] Mr. Cox requested that other corporations voluntarily disclose their illegal contributions to CREEP.

Also during the summer of 1973, Common Cause brought suit against CREEP, asking that all corporate contributions be revealed.[12] Common Cause won its suit; and that action, coupled with Mr. Cox's request for voluntary disclosures, was the first step in a process culminating in the conviction of eighteen corporations for violation of federal law prohibiting corporate political contributions.[13] Fines of $1,000 to $25,000 were levied.[14] The aftermath of Watergate saw the first federal prosecutions of Gulf Oil and other corporations for violation of the Corrupt Practices Act.

THE GULF OIL CORPORATION

Among the reasons for focusing on Gulf's actions, three are of prime importance. First, Gulf's criminal actions were expensive and elaborate, with at least $5 million of carefully laundered cash contributed to the campaign treasuries of hundreds of candidates for federal, state, and local offices.[15] Second, Gulf's actions were investigated extensively by government agencies and congressional committees, thus permitting detailed description and analysis. Third, Gulf's actions appear to be representative of a frequent type of corporate criminality.

Description of Gulf's Actions[16]

In about 1959, four of Gulf's top executives—William K. Whiteford, Gulf's chairman of the board and chief executive officer; Joseph Bounds, executive vice-president; Archie Gray, general counsel; and William T. Grummer, comptroller—became alarmed over what they perceived as "creeping encroachment"[17] by government toward the oil industry. They complained publicly about arbitrary oil import quotas, attacks against depletion allowances, government agencies unwilling to grant Gulf a fair hearing, and conflicting government regulations. In a pamphlet sent to stockholders and employees, it was argued:

> We have seen the development of a situation in which Gulf—and the industry—had been subjected to increasing attacks while in the political climate of our times, it has increasingly been denied a fair hearing.[18]

In that same pamphlet Gulf called upon employees and stockholders to "get involved"[19] in politics and announced the opening of a Government Relations office in Washington, DC.

The immediate problem confronting the Gulf executives committed to a more active political involvement was gathering the money needed for such an undertaking. Apparently aware of the Corrupt Practices Act, they initially attempted to gather voluntary contributions from Gulf executives. This legal "flower fund" scheme failed, and those involved decided to launder and then secretly distribute corporate funds to politicians.

Laundering: The Bahamas Connection

Money is laundered in an effort to mask its origins because its source does not want to be identified.[20] The laundering process typically involves sending money from its source to another location, usually a person and bank in a foreign country. The original money is then exchanged in the foreign country, and clean money is returned to its country of origin for dispersal.

William Whiteford, described in a later company investigation as "the dynamic and colorful Chairman of the Board and Chief Executive Officer of Gulf at the time,"[21] originally developed the idea of an off-the-books political fund. The plan was to be kept secret, even from the Mellon family, whose ancestors had founded Gulf, and from some people high in the Gulf hierarchy. People lower in the hierarchy whose participation was needed—for example, some people who set up the accounting procedures—sometimes also were kept in the dark or told only parts of the scope and purpose of the scheme.

Laundering of cash for the scheme was to occur at Bahamas Exploration, a nearly inactive Gulf subsidiary located in Nassau. Each year this subsidiary applied for and received a small number of exploration licenses, and occasionally it undertook exploratory surveys. Prior to 1959, Bahamas Exploration appears to have been a holding operation, spending only $100,000 annually to reserve a place for Gulf if significant deposits of petroleum or natural gas would be found in the Bahamas. Beginning in 1959 its budget multiplied as it was made part of an elaborate scheme to generate cash secretly.

William Viglia was an assistant comptroller responsible for accounting at several Bahamian subsidiaries, including Bahamas Exploration. In 1961, Executive Vice-President Joseph Bounds called him to Gulf's corporate headquarters in Pittsburgh. Mr. Bounds told him that funds would be coming down to the Bahamas and that he was to deliver some of this money to Bounds and some of it to the Gulf vice-president for governmental affairs in Washington. Mr. Viglia did as he was told, returned to Nassau, established the first of several bank accounts, and awaited instruction regarding return of the clean money to the United States. The money moved as follows:

> After receipt from Viglia of an envelope containing cash, Bounds locked it in the safe which [Chairman of the Board and Chief Executive Officer William] Whiteford had asked him to maintain in his office on the 31st floor of the Gulf Building. After a delivery, Bounds informed Whiteford . . . [who] . . . entered Bound's office during the latter's absence, opened the safe, removed the envelope, and left the safe open. The safe remained open and empty until another Viglia delivery, when the same procedures were followed.[22]

During a three-year period starting in about 1961, $669,000 was returned to the United States in this way. After Mr. Bounds retired in 1965, all money for political candidates was delivered directly to Claude Wild in Washington.

In 1959, Mr. Wild had been a legislative analyst for the Mid-Continent Oil and Gas Association. He was known to have extensive contacts with members of Congress and their aides when Gulf officials hired him to head their newly created Government Relations Office in Washington, D.C. The executives who hired him told him that Gulf had been "kicked around, knocked around by government"[23] and that Gulf intended to change that. They also told him that he would distribute a minimum of $200,000 each year to candidates, that such illegal corporate campaign contributions were "a part of life,"[24] and that Gulf merely would be joining other corporations in making such contributions. Nonetheless, he and Mr. Viglia apparently were quite conscious of the illegality of their actions, taking many precautions to shield them from outsiders:

> Viglia . . . never . . . [came] to Wild's offices . . . no records were maintained . . . when Wild needed funds he telephoned Viglia and Viglia delivered the cash . . . Wild and Viglia met at various points throughout the United States but never in a Gulf office.[25]

Distributing: The Washington Connection

Millions of dollars cannot be distributed by one person, especially in small amounts as was Gulf's custom. In Mr. Wild's words, it was "physically impossible for one man to handle that kind of money."[26] Consequently, he had help in distributing the money from three people in his own office, seven of his office's regional vice-presidents, and seven others, including Gulf employees and some personal friends. He personally handled nearly all payments to candidates for national office while his assistants handled those for state and local politicians.

Mr. Wild indicated that the only criterion for distributing these funds was that "the money be spent in the general interest of Gulf and the oil industry."[27] Of the $5 million spent, it is possible to identify the recipients of only $870,000. Mr. Wild declined to identify recipients on advice of counsel. Nonetheless, it is possible to construct the partial list contained in Table 6.1.

TABLE 6.1.   Organizations and Persons Known to Have Received Campaign Contributions From Gulf Corporate Funds, 1960–1972, in $ Amounts[a]

ORGANIZATIONS RECEIVING FUNDS	$ AMOUNT
CREEP	100,000
Republican Senate Committee	50,000
Democratic Committee Dinners	40,000
Republican Committee Dinners	80,000
Pennsylvania, State and Local Elections	75,000/yr.[b]
Texas, State and Local Elections	50,000/yr.[b]
California, State and Local Elections	15,000/yr.[b]
Louisiana, State and Local Elections	50,000/yr.[b]
Virginia, State and Local Elections	10,000/yr.[b]
New Mexico, State and Local Elections	10,000/yr.[b]
Mississippi, State and Local Elections	"sporadic"
Arkansas, State and Local Elections	"sporadic"

PERSONS RECEIVING FUNDS	$ AMOUNT
Walter Jenkins, aide to Senator Lyndon B. Johnson, Texas	50,000
Senator Henry Jackson, Washington	10,000
Carl Arnold, friend of Representative Wilbur Mills, Arkansas	15,000
Senator Hugh Scott, Pennsylvania	10,000/yr.[b]
Pat O'Connor, personal confidant of Senator Hubert H. Humphrey, Minnesota	25,000
Representative Richard Roudebush, Indiana	unknown amount of cash[c]
Senator Edwin Mechem, New Mexico	unknown amount of cash[c]
Senator Howard Cannon, Nevada	unknown amount of cash[c]
Governor William H. Avery, Kansas	unknown amount of cash[c]
George Bloom, Pennsylvania Utility Commissioner	unknown amount of cash[c]
Senator Howard Baker, Tennessee	2,000

TABLE 6.1   (Continued)

PERSONS RECEIVING FUNDS	$ AMOUNT
Representative Hale Boggs, Louisiana	unknown amount of cash[c]
Representative Melvin Price, Illinois	unknown amount of cash[c]
Representative Joe L. Evins, Tennessee	unknown amount of cash[c]
Representative Craig Hosmer, California	unknown amount of cash[c]
Representative Chet Holifield, California	unknown amount of cash[c]
Mr. Gerald, Adm. Assistant to Senator Allen Ellender, Louisiana	unknown amount of cash[c]
Adm. Assistant to Representative William C. Cramer, Florida	2,000
Senator William Brock, Tennessee	2,000
Representative John H. Heinz, Pennsylvania	2,000
Representative Frank M. Clark, Pennsylvania	2,000
Representative William S. Moorehead, Pennsylvania	1,000
Governor Milton Shapp, Pennsylvania	5,000
Raymond J. Broderick, candidate for Governor, 1970, Pennsylvania	3,500
Representative Jack Brooks, Texas	1,000
Governor Louie Nunn, Kentucky	1,000
Governor Ronald Reagan Campaign Committee, California	2,000
Governor Preston Smith, Texas	unknown amount of cash[c]
Estimated Total Known Contributions	870,000[d]

SPECIAL NOTE: There is no reliable evidence that the organizations and persons receiving Gulf funds knew of their corporate and consequently illegal origins. Organizations and individuals are identified only for purposes of suggesting the scope of Gulf's actions.

[a]Source for this information is *Securities and Exchange Commission* v. *Gulf Oil Corporation*, Civil Action No. 75-0324, United States District Court, District of Columbia, Report of The Special Review Committee of the Board of Directors of Gulf Oil Corporation, December 30, 1975, pp. 64–85.

[b]The exact number of years contributions were made was not specified. Total dollar amount estimates are based on the assumption that the amounts indicated were provided at least twice, a conservative estimate.

[c]The typical contribution appears to have been $2,000, as is apparent from the situations in which the amount given was known. For purposes of estimating the total amount of known contributions, the figure used was $1,000, a conservative estimate.

[d]This is a conservative estimate, as indicated in preceding notes b and c.

As can be seen from the table, the single largest known contribution was made to President Nixon's reelection committee (CREEP). The amount was $100,000, and its most important steps have been described as follows:

Mr. Lee Nunn ... came to Wild's office and told that the Committee to
Re-Elect the President would handle the 1972 Nixon Campaign outside
the normal Republican channels.... Nunn ... suggested that if Wild
wanted verification of Nunn's role in the effort he should get in touch with
Attorney General John Mitchell. Wild met with Mitchell in his office at
the Department of Justice and Mitchell indicated that ... [CREEP] ... was
a legitimate operation and that Mitchell had full confidence in Nunn.[28]

Wild then called Viglia, obtained $50,000 in cash, and delivered it to
Nunn. Some time later Secretary of Commerce Maurice Stans called
Wild and told him that a "kind of quota for large corporations of
around $100,000"[29] had been established. Wild again called Viglia and
subsequently delivered the additional money.

Table 6.1 also shows that Gulf contributions were not limited to
candidates for the presidency. Gulf funds were distributed to congressional campaign committees; to United States senators and representatives, their aides, and friends; and to candidates for state and local
office. Apparently, Gulf felt that not only had it been "kicked around,
knocked around" by federal government but by state and local government as well.

Disclosure: The Rediscovery of Deviance

Gulf's illicit activities were a well-kept secret despite the involvement of tens of Gulf employees and hundreds of recipients. Were it not
for the Watergate break-in there is no reason to believe the actions of
Gulf and hundreds of other corporations would have been disclosed.

Nor, we believe, would corporate contributions have been so widely
publicized and criticized were it not for Watergate. Gulf and other
corporations were tainted by their association with Watergate. Reac-
tions probably were stronger than they would have been in calmer
times.

Three quarters of a century ago the French sociologist Émile Durkheim (1858–1917) noted that "crime brings together upright con-
sciences and concentrates them. We have only to note what happens,
particularly in a small town, when some moral scandal has just been
committed."[30] Media-publicized scandals such as Watergate have
much the same effect in a mass society. Media coverage concentrates
people's moral perceptions and can lead to a reassertion of long-dor-
mant norms.

Media coverage of Watergate appeared to have had the effect of
reasserting the legitimacy of laws forbidding corporate campaign contributions. In the wake of the scandal, Henry Ford II called for changes
to "minimize the opportunity for influence peddling and buying."[31]

More than 90 percent of a national poll of Chambers of Commerce members wanted stricter laws and penalties to curb improper election practices.[32] Though there still was diversity on exactly what should be done, there was a reassertion of the belief that corporate campaign contributions were deviant, not just illegal:

> The business community had reason to be alarmed by the image it projected as details of corporate contributions to the Nixon re-election campaign became known. In mid-1973, at the peak of the Watergate investigations, a Gallup survey found that business ranked last among eight institutions measured in terms of public confidence and respect; an Opinion Research Corporation survey also measured a sharp decline in the percentage of those strongly supporting business. *The Wall Street Journal, Business Week,* and other periodicals published articles about draining public confidence in business, coupled with the growing cynicism that part of what Watergate signified—spying, sabotage, "dirty tricks"—was connected to cash supplied by big business.[33]

However, public concern about corporate political money was short-lived. As the media shifted their attention to gasoline shortages and inflation, corporations pushed for opportunities to help support political campaigns. In December of 1975 the Federal Election Commission ruled that corporate "political actions committees" (PACs) were legal, a ruling upheld by the Supreme Court in 1976.[34] PACs operate much like the flower fund Gulf's top executives tried to start in 1959. Corporations secure voluntary donations from management personnel. To facilitate donations, corporations provide "payroll deduction and check-off plans."[35] PACs then contribute these donations to selected politicians.

In 1976 legal PAC contributions were $6.8 million, triple what they had been in 1972.[36] In 1980 it was estimated that corporate PAC contributions totaled $50 million and likely will total at least $100 million in 1984.[37] A few short years after the Watergate scandal, corporate involvement in elections is not viewed as deviant.

ANALYSIS OF DEVIANCE AGAINST THE PUBLIC-AT-LARGE

In our analysis of corporate deviance against the public-at-large, we seek answers to the following question: what is it about life in and around large organizations that impels individuals to commit deviant acts? Analysis of Gulf's actions suggests that three organizational forces were important: (1) the availability of numerous essentially accurate rationalizations for deviance, (2) the limited information and responsibility characteristic of social roles in large organizations, and (3) the selection and training of loyal employees. We will review and consolidate these organizational forces and then examine the complementary interests of big business and big government.

Rationalizing Deviance

Rationalizations[38] are explanations for actions taken or planned. People use rationalizations to explain past actions to themselves and, if there are questions, to others. People also use rationalizations in advance of certain actions, literally permitting their release. These prebehavior rationalizations are especially important in permitting release of actions known to be improper or illegal. They are the reason a person provides, in advance of deviance, explanations as to why it is necessary and acceptable to engage in actions that otherwise would make one uncomfortable.

Corporate structures and environments provide executives with numerous essentially accurate rationalizations for deviance. In the case of Gulf, available rationalizations were so numerous and accurate that most individuals finding themselves in the same positions as Gulf's executives probably would have decided to violate the Corrupt Practices Act.

Gulf's elites could tell themselves that other corporations were doing what they were considering. They could describe illegal contributions as a routine part of corporate and political life. Making contributions appeared safe, for the portions of the federal Corrupt Practices Act applying to corporations had never been applied in its long existence. Failure to make contributions appeared risky, for other less inhibited corporations might gain advantages over Gulf.

Furthermore, the likelihood and consequences of detection were minor. Elites could note that efforts to hide the activity were likely to succeed. Even if they failed, however, not much would happen. The general public would not maintain a sustained interest in the issue. Stockholders were unlikely to react negatively. Government fines would undoubtedly be small. And the participants could defend their actions by saying that they were just filling their roles and did not directly benefit from their actions.

These rationalizations were essentially accurate. Gulf was at a disadvantage as compared to the over 300 other corporations known to have made illegal contributions. Disclosure was an accident attributable to politicians who used Gulf money carelessly. Members of the general public did not show sustained interest in corporate involvement in elections, with PAC contributions tripling in the three years following

Watergate. Stockholders were not upset, as stock prices increased in the months following disclosure.[39] Gulf was fined only $5,000. And, no person was harshly punished.

Social Roles in Large Organizations

A limited set of work-related expectations is associated with each position in a corporation. These expectations are narrowly defined and tend to resist pressures for change. Once deviant corporation actions have been created, therefore, they often seem to take on lives of their own. The deviant act is parceled out among a number of positions, each with no overall responsibility. People fit into these narrow roles rather comfortably.[40]

Most of the people who participated in Gulf's actions did not have, need, or probably want complete information or responsibility. They simply did what was defined for them as part of their job, something that was true for individuals at all levels of Gulf.

Consider the role of Gulf's comptrollers.[41] As can be seen in Table 6.2, three individuals followed the comptroller who helped launch Gulf's actions. None of the three had to make any difficult decisions, much less involve themselves in crime. All they were told is that they would receive requests for money from certain employees. All they did was write notes to treasurers, asking that these employees be provided the requested money.

TABLE 6.2.   **Persons Occupying Four Top Level Positions Within Gulf Oil, 1958–1973[a]**

CHIEF EXECUTIVE OFFICER AND CHAIRMAN OF THE BOARD	COMPTROLLER	TREASURER	GENERAL COUNSEL
William Whiteford[b] 1958–1965	William Grummer[b] 1958–1964	Horace Moorhead 1958–1972	Archie Gray[b] 1958–1960
E. D. Brockett 1965–1972	William Henry 1964–1966	Paul H. Weyrouch 1972–1973	David Searls 1960–1961
Robert Dorsey 1972–1973	Frank Anderson 1966–1968		Royce Savage 1961–1969
	Fred Deering 1968–1973		Merle Minks 1969–1973

[a]Source for this information is *Securities and Exchange Commission* v. *Gulf Oil Corporation*, Civil Action No. 75–0324, United States District Court, District of Columbia, Report of The Special Review Committee of the Board of Directors of Gulf Oil Corporation, December 30, 1975, pp. 64–85.
[b]Initiator of laundering and illegal campaign contributions operations.

Gulf's treasurers also knew and did little. All they were told was that the Bahamas Exploration account was "highly sensitive and confidential."[42] All they did was send checks to that account upon receipt of a note from a comptroller.

Tens of other Gulf employees engaged in similar actions, knowing or choosing to know very little, doing as they were told. John Brooks describes one man who delivered Gulf cash to a great many recipients:

> Most often the delivery would be at an airport or at the recipient's office, but occasionally it would be at the place suggestive of a desire for secrecy ... in 1970 he handed an envelope to Representative Richard L. Roudebush, of Indiana, ... in the men's washroom of a motel in Indianapolis. ... Time and again, asked ... whether he knew what was in the envelope he had delivered, he replied, "I do not," or "I have no knowledge." A minor figure ... apparently content to spin constantly above the cities, plains, and mountains of America, not knowing why, not wanting to know why ...[43]

Selecting and Training Loyal Employees

All organizations have sensitive and important secrets[44] and thus are dependent upon the loyalty of employees. Additionally, all organizations engage in actions that could prove embarrassing were they to be stripped of their organizational context and displayed in a public arena.

Organizations, therefore, select and train loyal employees. Selection involves searching applicants for signs of loyalty, with a major sign of loyalty being similar to the people who previously had proved to be loyal:

> Forces stemming from organizational situations ... promote social conformity as a standard for conduct ... managers choose others who can be "trusted." And thus they reproduce themselves in kind ... forces insisting that trust means total dedication and non-diffuse loyalty ... serve to exclude those ... who are seen as incapable of such single-minded attachment.[45]

Training of new organizational members involves verification of the loyalty of those selected. The technique includes gradual and piecemeal introduction to the corporation's sensitive and important secrets.[46] No one individual, especially initially, need know all or even most of what the corporation is doing. All that is required is a willingness to do one's job, to keep bits and pieces of secrets. With time, with sufficient verification of loyalty, as the need arises, loyal employees can be rewarded with promotion and thus exposure to more complete and important secrets.

Gulf's employees were the loyal products of these routine selection and training procedures. Rumor and limited evidence of criminality were widespread within Gulf. Comptrollers received cautious instructions to write notes to treasurers asking for money when told to do so by corporate subordinates. Treasurers receiving these notes sent money to the off-the-books account of a subsidiary that never did much of anything. Typists and clerks told jokes and stories of middle-level executives with "little black bags"[47] of Gulf money. No one went public.

Furthermore, large numbers of Gulf employees had access to over $5 million of essentially untraceable corporate funds. For obvious reasons, formal records were not kept, so there was no reliable method of verifying that laundered corporate funds actually had been delivered. Nevertheless, no one took Gulf's money:

> No evidence has been uncovered or disclosed which established that any officer, director, or employee of Gulf personally profited or benefited by or through any use of corporate funds for contributions, gifts, entertainment or other expenses related to political activity. Further ... [there is] no reason to believe or suspect that the motive of the employee or officer involved in such use of corporate funds was anything other than a desire to act solely in ... the best interests of Gulf and its shareholders.[48]

In sum: it appears that access to numerous essentially accurate rationalizations, limited information and responsibility characteristic of social roles in large organizations, and selection and training of loyal employees are among the elements of life in corporations that impel individuals in the direction of deviance.

A Model of Deviant Organizational Process Involving Elites[49]

Rationalizations, limited roles, and loyalty play an important part in facilitating deviant acts. Also important are the requirements placed on corporate elites. Top executives normally have more responsibilities than any one person can handle and a less rational basis for decision making than we tend to believe. Their information is limited, their definition of problems arbitrary, and, understandably, their decision making occasionally faulty. Instead of seeking until they find the best possible solution, they seek until they find a solution that meets their immediate needs. When failures occur, they seek again.

In the case of Gulf, the flower fund did not work, so another attempt was made. Politicians were provided laundered corporate funds across a twelve-year period. When this solution also failed, a third attempt, PACs, was initiated and appears to be working.

We now offer a model that shows the interplay among positions in Gulf and in many other cases. This is not a universal model of organizational behavior but rather a summary of those many instances when elites are involved in an activity that they recognized in advance as deviant.

1. Administrative coalitions define a company's problems and create an atmosphere supportive of a variety of solutions.
2. Innovative executives at or near the top of the corporate hierarchy respond to this atmosphere by advancing particular solutions. The innovators' intentions are to solve an important corporate problem in an easier or more effective manner.
3. Initiators involve a few key middle- and upper-level personnel in the project. These usually are people who have less power than the initiators, but whose active cooperation is fundamental to the success of their efforts.
4. Initiators circumvent the minority of individuals who cannot be trusted to remain loyal.
5. A larger number of lower-level employees are peripherally involved. These individuals have little information, so they do not know, or can choose not to know, the meaning of the corporate acts to which they contribute.
6. Corporate elites involved in initiating the action slowly become distant from it, giving day-to-day responsibility to middle-level managers. Ultimately, this delegation of responsibility shields them from obvious signs of involvement.
7. The activity becomes part of organizational life, and participants no longer question the informal role definitions supporting it.
8. New recruits find that the activity is a taken-for-granted part of their roles. They either comply or are circumvented.
9. The deviant activity continues until it is challenged by an outsider. Then a new definition of the problem and a new solution for it is sought.

Big Business and Big Government

We now turn our attention from internal corporate processes to external relations between corporations and their environments. In the case of political contributions, the most important environment obviously is government.

One view of big business–big government relations is adversarial. According to this pluralist perspective,[50] industry keeps a check on government, and government controls corporate excesses. In such a situation the public-at-large is protected from harmful corporate or governmental actions by the countervailing power of each institutional sphere.

The actions we have examined in this and earlier chapters suggest an alternative to pluralist images of big business–big government relations. Instead of viewing business and government as adversaries, we may find it more accurate to view them as colleagues sharing overlapping and essentially similar interests. President Eisenhower warned of the dangers of such a symbiotic relationship when, in his farewell address to the nation, he focused on the arms industry's relationship to government:

> This conjunction of an immense Military Establishment and a large arms industry is new in the American experience. The total influence—economic, political, even spiritual—is felt in every city, every statehouse, every office of the Federal Government. . . . We should never let the weight of this combination endanger our liberties or democratic processes.[51]

In the years since this address, there are clear signs that what was once a warning is now reality. Persons in top-level positions in government and business have much in common with one another.[52] They share common life-styles and values. They frequently exchange positions, moving between positions of power and responsibility in business and government. If there is difference between persons in government and business, it is that politicians lack direct access to corporate resources.

Government and business also need each other. A presidential attempt at voluntary price controls needs the cooperation of large corporations. Corporations need government assistance to provide hospitable economic environments or protect market segments from foreign competition. This regular contact and cooperation signals symbiotic rather than adversarial relations:

> The United States had moved well down the path toward a corporate state. Economic power is concentrated in the hands of a relatively few supercorporations. . . . Political power has shifted heavily into the hands of the executive branch of the federal government. . . . These two centers of economic and political power have developed a growing symbiosis.[53]

When looked at in this way, Gulf's political contributions emerge as part of the fabric of the corporate state. Gulf's actions were part of an exchange relationship in which each party expected to benefit. For the politicians who ran government, Gulf and other contributing corporations were solving a problem. They were providing access to corporate resources. Being a politician is costly, and money is fundamental to political survival. The grander the ambition or the higher the office, the more costly it is.

In exchange, politicians did not have to sell their votes or themselves. Gulf was not buying votes or people. All Gulf was paying politicians for was the predictability that all corporations seem to need to survive and prosper. Gulf's chief complaint was that inconsistent government regulation was making rational planning difficult. It was asking and paying for a more consistent set of regulations, ones that would permit the "calculable adjudication and administration"[54] fundamental to corporate capitalism. The precise content of the regulations frequently was less important than their predictability.[55]

SUMMARY AND CONCLUSION

This chapter examined corporate violations of the Corrupt Practices Act. We sketched the origins of laws forbidding corporate contributions and traced their enforcement following the Watergate break-in. We described and then analyzed the actions of one corporate violator, Gulf Oil.

The essential explanation for Gulf's actions has been organizational. We have suggested that it is possible and enlightening to view this episode in organizational rather than purely individualistic terms. Indeed, that has been the theme of the last four chapters. Because of this single theme, we will use this summary section to establish an important point.

Responsibilities of Individuals in Large Organizations

An organizational focus does not excuse individuals or suggest they have no choice. The individuals involved in the episodes we have examined generally knew that their actions were improper, as evidenced by their efforts to hide them. They had choices and could have refused to become involved. They also could have alerted outsiders to deviant corporate actions, thus eliminating the need for personal involvement. Hence we do not consider an organizational focus either a defense or an excuse.

An organizational focus instead is an explanation for the actions of individuals in large organizations. It emphasizes the overriding importance of corporate resources and structures. It argues that some actions could not have occurred were it not for membership in large corporations. It stresses the explanatory significance of extra-individualistic forces and events.

Social scientists search for extra-individualistic explanations of human action. In attempting to explain the street crime of the poor, sociologists regularly isolate poverty and racism as prime causal factors.[56] These two factors surely are among the extra-individualistic forces responsible for their actions.

Likewise, organizational forces are among the reasons executives initiate and employees carry out deviant corporate acts. But such forces are not an excuse or defense. Indeed, the frequent wealth and privilege of the individuals who initiate corporate deviance perhaps make them more deserving of punishment than the person involved in desperate and unrewarding street crime. This, however, raises the issue of control, the focus of the next two chapters.

ANNOTATED SELECTED READINGS

Alexander, Herbert E. *Financing the 1972 Election.* Lexington, MA: Lexington Books, 1976. Detailed history of financing of the 1972 election, including the impact of Watergate, sources and disbursement of political funds, and the changing legal structure.

Bolton, David. *The Grease Machine: The Lockheed Papers.* New York: Harper & Row, 1977. Detailed and well-written account of the Lockheed Corporation's bribes of hundreds of foreign officials in tens of nations.

Brooks, John. "The Bagman." In Rosabeth Moss Kanter and Barry A. Stein, eds., *Life in Organizations: Workplaces as People Experience Them.* New York: Basic Books, 1979. Pp. 363–372. Description and some analysis of Gulf's illegal actions.

Hougan, Jim. "The Business of Buying Friends." In John M. Johnson and Jack D. Douglas, eds., *Crime at the Top: Deviance in Business and the Professions.* Philadelphia: Lippincott, 1978. Pp. 196–226. Somewhat superficial account of the Lockheed Corporation's bribes of foreign officials.

Jaworski, Leon. *The Right and the Power: The Prosecution of Watergate.* New York: Pocket Books, 1977. Description of the prosecution of the individuals and corporations involved in Watergate. Useful throughout, with pages 342–349 providing a concise summary of the executives and corporations involved and what happened to them.

Report of the Special Review Committee of the Board of Directors of Gulf Oil
Corporation. *Securities and Exchange Commission, Plaintiff* v. *Gulf Oil Corporation, Claude C. Wild, Jr., Defendants.* Civil Action No. 75–0324, United
States District Court for the District of Columbia, December 30, 1975. Much
of our description and analysis of Gulf's actions in this chapter was based
upon this report. You can obtain a copy in the same way we did. We wrote
to: General Counsel, Gulf Oil Corporation, 439 Seventh Avenue, Pittsburgh,
PA 15230.

Sobel, Lester A., ed. *Money and Politics: Contributions, Campaign Abuses & the
Law.* New York: Facts on File, Inc., 1974. A very detailed compendium of
finance-related activities and violations surrounding the 1972 election. Useful for identifying people, events, and sequences. Offers little interpretation.

NOTES

1. Edwin M. Epstein, "The Emergence of Political Action Committees," in
   Herbert E. Alexander, ed., *Political Finance* (Beverly Hills: Sage, 1979),
   p. 160.
2. See Herbert E. Alexander, *Political Financing* (Minneapolis: Burgess
   Publishing, 1972), pp. 25–27.
3. Materials for this section are derived from: Alexander, *Political Financing;* Perry Belmont, *Return to Secret Party Funds* (New York: Putnam's,
   1927, rpt. in New York by Arno Press, 1974); Louise Overbacker, *Money
   in Elections* (New York: Macmillan, 1932, rpt. in New York by Arno
   Press, 1974); Lester A. Sobel, ed., *Money and Politics: Contributions, Campaign Abuses & the Law* (New York: Facts on File Inc., 1974).
4. Overbacker, *Money,* p. 175.
5. Quoted in Belmont, *Return,* p. 37.
6. Belmont, *Return,* p. 47.
7. Overbacker, *Money,* p. 294.
8. One judge, probably sharing some of the mixed feelings of his fellow
   citizens, saw no distinction between political expenditures by citizens and
   those by corporations. He said in his decision:
   I infer that the power company was attacked, and it is asking too much
   of human nature to expect the corporation not to defend itself.
       On the other hand, if the corporation set out to corrupt the electorate,
   it must certainly be punished. . . .
   The judge found the latter to be the case, although there was no specifica-
   tion of the criteria used to determine that this corporate contribution was
   corrupt (Overbacker, *Money,* p. 337).

9. *Securities and Exchange Commission, Plaintiff* v. *Gulf Oil Corporation, Claude C. Wild, Jr., Defendants,* Civil Action No. 75–0324, United States District Court for the District of Columbia, Report of the Special Review Committee of the Board of Directors of Gulf Oil Corporation, December 30, 1975, p. 3. This document will hereafter be identified as SEC, *Report.*
10. Carl Bernstein and Robert Woodward, *All the President's Men* (New York: Warner Paperback Library, 1975), p. 16.
11. For a discussion, see Leon Jaworski, *The Right and the Power: The Prosecution of Watergate* (New York: Pocket Books, 1977), p. 21.
12. SEC, *Report,* p. 7.
13. The eighteen convicted corporations, most of which pleaded guilty, were American Airlines, American Shipbuilding, Ashland Oil, Associated Milk Producers, Braniff Airways, Carnation Company, Diamond International, Goodyear Tire, HMS Electric, Gulf Oil, LBC & W, Incorporated, Lehigh Valley Co-op, Minnesota Mining, National By-Products, Northrup Aviation, Phillips Petroleum, Time Oil, and Ratrie, Robbins, and Schweitzer (Jaworski, *The Right,* pp. 344–345). In addition, three hundred other corporations were reported to have made illegal contributions. See Marshall B. Clinard, *Illegal Corporate Behavior* (Washington, DC: Government Printing Office, 1979), p. 200.
14. Jaworski, *The Right,* pp. 344–345.
15. SEC, *Report,* pp. 51–52.
16. This section is based upon SEC, *Report,* pp. 1–91, 199–298.
17. SEC, *Report,* p. 62.
18. Ibid.
19. Ibid.
20. For a discussion of laundering in the context of "Watergate," see Bernstein and Woodward, *All The President's Men,* pp. 38 ff.
21. SEC, *Report,* p. 43.
22. Ibid.
23. Ibid., p. 63.
24. Ibid.
25. Ibid., p. 65.
26. Ibid., p. 66.
27. Ibid.
28. Ibid., p. 70.
29. Ibid., p. 71.
30. Émile Durkheim, *The Division of Labor in Society,* trans. by George Simpson (Glencoe, IL: Free Press, 1960), p. 102.
31. Herbert E. Alexander, *Financing the 1972 Election* (Lexington, MA: Lexington Books, 1976), p. 457.
32. Ibid., p. 458.
33. Ibid., p. 457.
34. Discussion of PACs is based upon Jonathan Tumin, "How to Bury Liberals," *The New Republic,* May 24, 1980, pp. 13–15.
35. Ibid., p. 14.
36. Herbert E. Alexander, *Financing the 1976 Elections* (Washington, DC: Congressional Quarterly Press, 1979). p. 544.

37. Tumin, "How to Bury," p. 14.
38. The imagery and vocabulary advanced in our discussion of rationalization is from Gresham Sykes and David Matza, "Techniques of Neutralization: A Theory of Delinquency," *American Sociological Review* 22 (1957): 644–670.
39. John Brooks, "The Bagman," in Rosabeth Moss Kanter and Barry A. Stein, eds., *Life in Organizations: Workplaces as People Experience Them* (New York: Basic Books, 1979), p. 372.
40. For a discussion of social order in large organizations, see Richard Hall, *Organizations: Structure and Process,* 2d ed. (Englewood Cliffs, NJ: Prentice Hall, 1977), pp. 26 ff.
41. SEC, *Report,* pp. 46–52.
42. Ibid., p. 223.
43. Brooks, "The Bagman," p. 367.
44. For an early discussion of this point, see Max Weber, *On Law in Economy and Society,* ed. and annotated by Max Rheinstein, trans. by Edward Shils and Max Rheinstein (New York: Simon & Schuster, 1967), pp. 334–335.
45. Rosabeth Moss Kanter, *Men and Women of the Corporation* (New York: Basic Books, 1977), p. 68.
46. All of the persons with access to Gulf's sensitive and important criminal secrets had served long corporate apprenticeships. See SEC, *Report,* pp. 242–266.
47. Ibid., p. 223.
48. Ibid., pp. 216–217.
49. See Chapter 1 for the theoretical basis for this model.
50. See Neal Shover, "The Criminalization of Corporate Behavior: Federal Surface Coal Mining," in Gilbert Geis and Ezra Stotland, eds., *White-Collar Crime* (Beverly Hills, Sage Publications, 1980), pp. 98–125.
51. Quoted in Seymour Melman, *Pentagon Capitalism: The Political Economy of War* (New York: McGraw-Hill, 1970), p. 237.
52. See C. Wright Mills, *The Power Elite* (New York: Oxford U.P., 1956); Michael Useem, "Studying the Corporation and the Corporate Elite," *The American Sociologist* 14 (May 1979): 97–107; Gwen Moore, "The Structure of a National Elite Network," *American Sociological Review* 44 (October 1979); 673–692.
53. Daniel R. Fusfeld, "The Rise of the Corporate State in America," *Journal of Economic Issues* 6 (March 1972): 1. See also Arthur S. Miller, *The Modern Corporate State: Private Governments and the American Constitution* (Westport, CT: Greenwood, 1976).
54. Max Weber, *General Economic History,* trans. by F. N. Knight (New York: Collier Books, 1961), p. 208, cited in Shover, "Federal Surface Coal Mining."
55. See Shover, "Federal Surface Coal Mining."
56. See Jeffrey H. Reiman, *The Rich Get Richer and the Poor Get Prison: Ideology, Class and Criminal Justice* (New York: Wiley, 1979).

THREE

Controlling
corporate
deviance

Non penetrating controls

Under any economic, social, or political system, individuals, business firms, and organizations in general are subject to lapses from efficient, rational, law-abiding, virtuous, or otherwise functional behavior. [Therefore,] lest the misbehavior feed on itself and lead to general decay, society must be able to marshal from within itself forces which will make as many of the faltering actors as possible revert to the behavior required for its proper functioning.
—*Albert O. Hirschman* [1]

Evidence presented in the last four chapters suggests that business corporations violate the rights of their intended beneficiaries. Thousands of owners lost millions of dollars in the wake of the Equity Funding Fund scandal.[2] Many lost their health—and some their lives —as employees of corporations such as Johns-Manville and Pittsburgh Corning.[3] Still others, among them large and prominent electrical utilities, paid millions of dollars in excessive costs to other large and prominent organizations, among them General Electric and Westinghouse.[4] And following Watergate, millions were troubled by the political contributions of Gulf and other corporations.[5]

Preview of the Chapter

This chapter will describe and evaluate alternative ways to control such corporate deviance. We begin by identifying two major types of control mechanism: nonpenetrating and penetrating. Then we direct attention to nonpenetrating control and three of its most important applications. In the next chapter we continue our examination of control, focusing on penetrating mechanisms.

We will show that a wide variety of possibly effective nonpenetrating and penetrating mechanisms have been tried. They range from giving beneficiaries choices to imposing fines and jail sentences. In evaluating them, we will illustrate why control is difficult regardless of the particular mechanism used.

Specifically, we will show that each control mechanism has important preconditions that must be met for it to be effective. Typically, these preconditions are not met. Large corporations, therefore, are only weakly controlled by the people and organizations in their environment.

NONPENETRATING AND PENETRATING CONTROLS

Nonpenetrating controls assume that corporate actions can be influenced from the outside by selectively rewarding and punishing the corporation. They do not try to influence directly internal corporate workings. They avoid mandating specific changes in corporate structures, procedures, or personnel. Instead, these mechanisms seek levers outside the corporation that may cause it to make necessary changes itself. The parallel for controlling individual burglars is to ignore their psychological condition and, instead, to try to change their environments and behaviors by providing employment or strengthening punishment.

This approach assumes that with proper external incentives, burglars and deviant corporations will find better channels for their efforts. It also assumes that too little currently is known about how to alter the inner workings of burglars' minds or corporations' structures. Therefore, it proposes that the best available controls are nonpenetrating mechanisms that change environments to make violators change their actions in the future and to make potential violators remain conforming.

On the other hand, penetrating mechanisms assume there are features of a corporation's structure and personnel, just as there are aspects of a burglar's life experiences and personality, that increase the likelihood of deviance. They assume also that these aspects can be changed. In the case of the corporation, changes might include the way members of the Board of Directors are elected, how lower level managers are promoted, or how often people are transferred from job to job or city to city. Other important changes might include the way top management is informed of the behavior of subordinates and how it is accountable to the Board of Directors. If these patterns contribute to corporate deviance and if they can be changed by outsiders, then penetrating the organization and changing them possibly can reduce deviance.

NONPENETRATING CONTROLS

Nonpenetrating controls can attempt to change corporate environments in a variety of ways. To the authors, the three most important nonpenetrating controls are those that give choices to beneficiaries, facilitate adverse publicity, and impose stiff fines.[6]

Beneficiary-Choice Systems

One method for controlling corporations is to permit free market forces to operate unfettered. This mechanism is especially advocated by corporate spokespersons.[7] Their argument runs along the following lines. Every corporation has outsiders who have an interest in the corporation because they are either owners, employees, customers, or the general public. These beneficiaries are protected because they can choose from among competing corporations. Furthermore, the separate and uncoordinated choices they make can penalize the corporation that fails to serve them. According to corporate spokespersons, therefore, a beneficiary choice system forces corporations to serve their beneficiaries and penalizes those corporations that are deviant.

In the case of customers, for instance, "the customer is always right" is based on the idea that customers get what they want because they pay the bills and, therefore, can buy elsewhere if they are dissatisfied. The same process is said to operate for other beneficiaries. A corporation whose profits are too low will be pressured to increase its profits because investors can refuse to invest in it. And a company having low wages or maintaining obviously unsafe working conditions may be unable to attract or retain qualified personnel.

Though this argument has its critics, prevailing American beliefs extol competition as working in the best interests of beneficiaries by giving them choices. It commonly is argued or at least assumed that giving stockholders, employees, and customers a free choice about whether to deal with a particular corporation or one of its competitors is a powerful control on corporate actions.

Preconditions

However, the obvious attraction of letting people choose what they want must be tempered by recognition of preconditions for such systems to work. These preconditions are crucial. To the extent that they are met, corporations possibly can be forced to serve their normative beneficiaries. Conversely, to the extent that they go unmet, corporations are free to violate beneficiaries' rights. We now will provide a detailed evaluation of these preconditions, first by listing them and then by discussing them.

1. *Many corporations must offer* the goods or services or a reasonable substitute.
2. *These offering corporations must compete* to be chosen by the beneficiary.
3. *Additional corporations must be able to enter* the field if existing ones fail.
4. *Beneficiaries must exercise choices.* They must know choices exist and be willing and able to change allegiance.
5. *Resources must depend on choices.* Choices made by beneficiaries must determine whether the corporation gets the resources necessary for its existence.

Many Corporations Must Offer

For choices to exist, many corporations must be offering goods or services. Often this is not the case. First, having multiple corporations is considered an inefficient way to provide electricity, cable television, and telephone service. The corporations that provide these and other goods and services are considered "natural monopolies."

There are many other monopolies and oligopolies not considered "natural." For example, choice between corporations is not great for people buying breakfast cereal, chewing gum, or sewing machines. The extent that choice is limited is illustrated by Table 7.1, which shows the percentage of shipments in selected industries for the four, eight, twenty, and fifty largest firms in each industry. In the breakfast cereal industry, for example, 90 percent of shipments are made by the four largest firms, and 98 percent by the eight largest.

TABLE 7.1. Shares of Total Values of Shipments Accounted for by the Four, Eight, Twenty, and Fifty Largest Companies in Selected Industries, 1972

Industry	PERCENT OF TOTAL VALUE OF SHIPMENTS ACCOUNTED FOR BY THE— LARGEST COMPANIES				Note: Total Number of Companies
	4	8	20	50	
General breakfast foods	90	98	99	100	34
Electric lamps	90	94	98	99+	103
Chewing gum	87	98	100	100	15
Household refrigerators and freezers	85	98	99+	100	30
Sewing machines	84	92	97	99+	NA
Chocolate and cocoa products	74	88	99	100	39
Roasted coffee	65	79	92	97	162
Soap and other detergents	62	74	85	92	577
Cookies and crackers	59	69	83	93	257
Men's and boys' underwear	49	71	91	99+	94
Petroleum refining	31	56	84	96	152
Frozen fruits and vegetables	29	43	69	91	136
Burial caskets	25	34	47	63	474
Sausage and prepared meats	19	26	38	54	1207
Book publishing	19	31	56	77	1120

Source: U.S. Bureau of the Census, Census of Manufacturers, 1972., Special Report.
Series: *Concentration Ratios on Manufacturing* MC 72 (SR)-2 (Washington, D.C.: U.S. Government Printing Office, 1975) Table 8, pp. 165–240.

In sum, although an abundance of corporations is crucial for the beneficiary-choice model of control, most beneficiaries have few corporations from which to choose. The first precondition for the successful operation of beneficiary-choice system thus often goes unmet.

These Offering Corporations Must Compete

It is not sufficient for beneficiary-choice controls that there be many corporations offering a good or service. The many organizations must act in ways that will attract beneficiaries away from one another. McDonald's must try to attract customers from Burger King, and General Electric must try to take customers from Westinghouse.

Corporations do compete for the favor of beneficiaries in some situations, although in others they do not. The tendency, however, appears to be for competition to diminish over time because corporations learn to accommodate to one another. One of the authors of this book observed subtle cooperation while he worked for a large auto manufacturer. A competitor of the author's firm had lowered a car price, winning significant sales as a result. People were buying the less expensive competitive car.

The response of the author's firm was summarized in an internal memorandum that described the situation and indicated that nothing would be done. It was assumed that the competitor would realize that to continue the lower price soon would force the author's company to lower its prices as well. Then with both companies selling at the lower price, both would be hurt. The competitor apparently perceived this, too, for with sales still high, it nevertheless raised prices to the previous level. An accommodation was reached without conspiracy and without apparent illegality.

However, we need not rely upon our own experiences for evidence of lack of competition. Nor should we assume that most accommodations are legal. Numerous early studies, Sutherland's *White-Collar Crime* among them,[8] reported that price-fixing was common. More recently, Marshall B. Clinard reported that price-fixing is frequent "in a wide variety of industries, including paper goods, electrical wiring, apparel, resins used to make paint, citrus fruit, computers, beer, plywood, armored car services, photography, and toilet seats...."[9]

Additional Corporations Must Be Able to Enter

Even if many corporations were competing, beneficiaries still would be served poorly if the corporations did not provide what beneficiaries want. The sheer organizational momentum of corporations already in business frequently precludes them from responding to change. American automobile manufacturers, for example, continued to build large cars after it was clear to foreign manufacturers that the "gas guzzler" was a thing of the past. Similarly, it was McDonald's and Kentucky

Fried Chicken, not established Howard Johnson's, that innovated fast-food outlets.[10] Newcomers to a market, thus, may be the only ones likely to offer desired goods or services.

This need for newcomers poses problems for beneficiary-choice systems. Entry by new firms now is essentially impossible in many economic sectors, though this has not always been the case. For example, in 1904 the auto industry had 121 competing firms. Entry for new firms was easy. "Few of the producers were endowed with more than meager resources; but both technological and financial factors made entrance into the business extremely easy...."[11] Henry Ford first entered the business by creating the Detroit Automobile Company in 1898 with $10,000 of investors' capital.[12] However, even "tiny" American Motors in 1975 had to spend $89 million just for automotive capital expenditures.[13] These costs make the chances for a new corporation's successfully starting production today slim indeed.[14]

Similarly, new products like home fire alarms or pocket calculators begin with many firms entering the market, but their numbers quickly decline, and entry by newcomers becomes increasingly difficult. Only in low capital industries such as massage parlors and TV repairs is the entry of newcomers likely. In other cases, this precondition of the beneficiary-choice model goes unmet.

Beneficiaries Must Exercise Choices

Choices that do exist must be recognized and used by beneficiaries. Only if their opportunity to choose is taken, can consumers turn choice into effective control. For example, the McDonnell-Douglas DC–10 has one of the worst civil aviation safety records. In 1974 a cargo door flew out of a DC–10, and 345 people were killed.[15] And in 1979 a DC–10 carrying 272 passengers crashed after losing an engine on takeoff.[16] Still, many passengers show up at the assigned time, and if they end up in a DC–10, they may silently hope that their flight will be safe. Even in the face of available options, these people fail to exercise choice because the options appear too time-consuming or inconvenient to discover and use.

Resources Must Depend on Choices

This final precondition requires that no alternative source of funds come to the rescue if beneficiaries flee. For a beneficiary choice system to work, a corporation cannot be insulated from a harsh fate if its customers, employees, or investors desert it.

However, corporations enjoy considerable insulation from the effects of negative decisions by beneficiaries. At the Pittsburgh-Corning asbestos plant in Tyler, Texas, workers routinely quit after only short periods of work because asbestos dust drove them away.[17] But willing replacements were found quickly, and the plant operated despite the rapid turnover. Workers did exercise choice, but had no effect on the Tyler factory.

This also is frequently the case when customers desert large corporations. By 1970, for example, Lockheed Aircraft was hopelessly in debt.[18] A major problem was its Tristar jumbo jet, which had not been as well received by commercial airline companies as the Boeing 747 and, ironically, the McDonnell-Douglas DC–10. But Congress rescued Lockheed with a $250 million loan guarantee, simultaneously preserving the company and insulating it from the effects of beneficiary-choice.

Evaluating Beneficiary-Choice Systems

Beneficiary-choice control relies on the simple assumption that corporate responses to changing economic environments are quick, predictable, rational, and income-maximizing. As taught in civics courses, the American economy is a collection of competing corporations offering their stock, goods and services, and employment to choosy outsiders. Beneficiaries make their choices from among competitors, and competitors adjust accordingly.

However, American experience suggests that choice often is ineffective as a mechanism for regulating corporate behavior and preventing deviance. Corporations seldom suffer from adverse decisions by their normative beneficiaries. As we have shown, the beneficiary-choice model is weakened because too few sellers are in a market, existing sellers do not compete, new competitors are unavailable, consumers do not exercise the available choices, and corporations are insulated by the depth of their alternative resources. It, therefore, seems unlikely that beneficiary-choice significantly controls corporate deviance.

CONTROL BY PUBLICITY

Corporations attempt to portray themselves as responsible community members. They need to be seen as legitimate, so they spend considerable amounts of time and money creating responsible public images.[19] Because they attach such importance to building and maintaining these images, negative publicity is a possible mechanism for controlling deviance.

For instance, agencies such as the Federal Trade Commission (FTC) and the Food and Drug Administration (FDA) can require corporations to correct misleading advertisements publicly.[20] These corrective advertisements should alter corporate reputations because they are admissions that corporations knowingly lied to consumers. It is not unreasonable to assume that corporations will avoid deviance in order to avoid such publicity.

News reports of corporate deviance also damage public images. Corporations, therefore, may try to avoid deviant behaviors thought likely to result in unfavorable news reports. Consider this recent observation by Marshall Clinard:

> Conversations with numerous federal and state enforcement officials revealed that possible publicity about law violations in the mass media is probably the most feared consequence of sanctions imposed on corporations. . . . Corporations generally do not wish to risk the publicity certain to arise from a prolonged court case or the imposition of a civil or criminal penalty.[21]

However, negative publicity can be effective only to the extent that certain preconditions are met.[22] If corrective advertisements are to be deterrents by reducing sales of falsely advertised products, they must be directed toward audiences originally misled. If news reports are to have an impact on corporate reputations, they must frequently and prominently link specific corporations with particular episodes of deviance.[23]

Corrective Advertising, The FTC, and STP[24]

The Federal Trade Commission (FTC) was created by Congress in 1914 to maintain a free market system. This includes prevention of false or deceptive advertisements lest they give unfair advantage to deceptive corporations. FTC rules permit fines of up to $10,000 per day for infractions, cease and desist orders, and public corrections of false advertisements.

STP is a marketer of oil additive, gas additives, air filters, and other automotive products. As part of its advertising in the early 1970s, STP falsely claimed its oil additive was more slippery than motor oil and thus reduced breakdowns by reducing friction. As an illustration of the superior slipperiness of STP, consumers were shown how easy it was to lift the working end of a screwdriver dipped in motor oil. Then they were shown how a screwdriver dipped in STP could not be lifted, presumably because it was more slippery than motor oil alone. Other claims, as with reducing breakdowns, also were false. In 1978 the FTC ordered STP to cease and desist from representing directly or by implication that any STP oil product

1. Prevents cars that use it from experiencing mechanical breakdowns or from requiring repairs.
2. Cures or remedies mechanical malfunctions.
3. Eliminates friction or wear or is required to protect against friction or wear.
4. Acts or performs like, or has the effect of, antifreeze in the oil. . . .
5. Is required in order to obtain lubrication from motor oil.
6. Is more slippery than motor oil alone.[25]

Similar orders applied to the company's gas additive and oil filters.

After negotiations between the FTC and STP, the company agreed to pay a $500,000 fine and spend $200,000 to place notices correcting the misrepresentations contained in its original advertisements. Following are the publications where original false advertisements and corrective notices appeared:

ORIGINAL ADS APPEARED IN	CORRECTIVE NOTICES APPEARED IN
Auto Aftermarket News	Barron's
Auto News	Business Week
Car & Driver	Esquire
Field & Stream	Forbes
Hot Rod	Guns and Ammo
Mechanix Illustrated	Harvard Business Review
Motor Age	National Geographic
Motor Trend	Newsweek
Playboy	New York Times
Popular Mechanics	People
Popular Science	Time Business Edition
Road & Track	U.S. News & World Report
Scientific American	Wall Street Journal
Service Station Management	Washington Post

The publications shown on these two lists are read by a significantly different clientele. The effect of the corrective advertisements on public perceptions or sales therefore was minimal. Few of the auto enthusiasts reading STP ads in auto or sports journals also read STP admissions in the primarily financial publications where the corrective notices were placed.

In agreeing to the preceding settlement, the FTC argued that corrective advertisements were not intended to alert consumers to false advertising by STP. The FTC believed that corrective advertising in primarily financial publications would give the business community a message about the consequences of false advertising. But the message to the financial community may not have been the one the FTC officially intended. After all, the FTC had made STP tell people who do not buy its product that it had lied to people who do buy its products. The message more likely received by corporations is the one described by humorist Art Buchwald:

> We are now in the offices of the Deal, Rehobeth and Gluckstein advertising agency where they are making a presentation to J. B. Rabbit, president of LS & D Company, who has just been ordered by the FTC to spend a million dollars to inform the public that it was misled by claims that an LS & D coffee ground additive would give people 20 extra miles to the gallon. "First we need a catchy slogan. How's this: "Anyone who put LS & D coffee grounds in his motor ought to have his head examined"?
>
> "That's a good slogan?" "Wait, J. B. The FTC didn't say where we had to put the ads. We've worked out a media plan. One third for newspapers, one third for magazines and one third for television. We'll place full-page ads in *The New York Herald Tribune, The New York Journal American, The New York Sun, The New York World Telegram* and *The Long Island Daily Press.*"
>
> "But those papers don't exist any more."
>
> "That's for the FTC to find out."
>
> "Where are you going to put the commercials?"
>
> "On the . . . Howard Cosell Variety Show."
>
> "Is that still on the air?"
>
> "Only in Bangladesh."[26]

STP customers who read the original ads are only a bit more likely than their LS & D counterparts to have had their misinformation corrected. Most did not read the corrective ads, nor were their perceptions or buying of this product changed. At least in the context of this episode, corrective advertisement was an ineffective control mechanism.

News Reports

News reports of corporate deviance can be effective only if they frequently and prominently link specific corporations to particular episodes of deviance. It they are not frequent or prominent or if corporations are not identified by name, then there is little possibility of using media publicity to control corporate deviance.

Although media coverage of corporate crime has been infrequently studied, there have been studies that provide useful comparisons of newspaper coverage of two price-fixing episodes.[27] We will review their findings because they appear to be representative of news reports of corporate deviance.

The Price-Fixing Episodes

On February 6, 1961, prosecution of the "most serious violation of the antitrust laws since the time of their passage at the turn of the century"[28] was completed in a federal courtroom in Philadelphia. As can be seen in Table 7.2, the illegal actions were discovered following a nineteen-month grand jury investigation, which resulted in criminal indictments of twenty-nine corporations and forty-five individuals. Indicted corporations[29] pleaded guilty and were fined a total of $1.8 million. Individual defendants entered *nolo contendere* pleas, were found guilty, and were fined a total of $137,000. Seven defendants served brief jail terms.

On November 30, 1976, prosecution of the folding carton industry price-fixing conspiracy, "as serious as any . . . during the first eighty-six years of the Sherman Act,"[30] was completed in a federal courtroom in Chicago. As also can be seen in Table 7.2, the conspirators used a variety of techniques to maintain existing market structures illegally during a thirty-year period. Their illegal actions were discovered following a nineteen-month grand jury investigation, which resulted in criminal indictments of twenty-three corporations and fifty individuals. The indicted corporations entered *nolo contendere* pleas, were found guilty, and then fined $1.1 million. Individual defendants also entered *nolo contendere* pleas and were found guilty. They were fined a total of $348,000, and fifteen were sentenced to, and served, brief jail terms.

Newspaper Coverage of the Cases

Two surveys of newspaper coverage of the 1961 heavy electrical equipment industry price-fixing case were undertaken. The first followed guilty pleas by corporate defendants, finding that

> sixteen percent [of the newspapers surveyed] . . . placed the story on page one, each with a single column heading . . . eleven percent used less than a column of print on an inside page . . . forty-three percent used less than half a column on an inside page . . . thirty percent . . . omitted any reference to the story.[31]

TABLE 7.2.   Selected Dimensions of the 1961 Heavy Electrical Equipment Industry and 1976 Folding Carton Industry Price-Fixing Cases

DIMENSION	1961 CASE[a]	1976 CASE[b]
Modus Operandi	minimize telephone calls; use plain envelopes for mailing; travel separately; public meeting places	minimize telephone calls; use plain envelopes for mailing; travel separately; public meeting places
Purpose	maintain existing market structure	maintain existing market structure
Duration	at least 30 years	at least 30 years
Annual Sales	$1.7 billion	$1.7 billion
Method of Securing Indictments	19-month grand jury investigation	18-month grand jury investigation
Nature of Indictments	criminal	criminal
Number of Corporate Defendants	29	23
Number of Individual Defendants	45	50
Pleas Entered by Corporate Defendants	guilty	nolo contendere
Pleas Entered by Individual Defendants	nolo contendere	nolo contendere
Total Corporate Fines	$1.8 million	$1.1 million
Total Individual Fines	$137,000	$348,200
Percent Individual Defendants Sentenced To Jail	15% (7 of 45)	36% (15 of 47)

[a]Source: Gilbert Geis, "White-Collar Crime: The Heavy Electrical Equipment Antitrust Cases of 1961," in M. David Ermann and Richard J. Lundman, eds. *Corporate and Governmental Deviance* (New York: Oxford U.P., 1978), pp. 59–79.
[b]Source: Jeffrey Sonnenfeld and Paul R. Lawrence, "Why do Companies Succumb to Price Fixing?" *Harvard Business Review* (July–August 1978): 145–157.

The second survey of leading newspapers followed sentencing of corporate and individual defendants and found that

forty-five percent of the newspapers in the survey kept the story of the sentencing off the first page. Fewer than a handful ... mentioned the names of any of the sentenced corporations other than General Electric and Westinghouse, and most of the papers devoted substantially all their headline space and coverage to the executives who received prison sentences. None of the newspapers emphasized the *corporations* were actually guilty of committing *crimes*. The language of criminality—words like "guilty," "sentences," and "criminal"—was generally reserved for the executives. More neutral language—words like "proceedings," "antitrust suits," and "penalties"—was employed in reference to corporate defendants.[32]

Replicative surveys of leading newspapers followed sentencing in the 1976 folding-carton case.[33] It was found that newspaper articles were less frequent, less prominent, and equally inexplicit in linking particular corporations with criminality. Despite Watergate and other social changes, newspaper coverage of the 1976 case was slightly less complete than it had been in 1961.

Evaluating Control by Publicity

The idea of control by publicity is based on the assumption that corporations try to maintain positive public images and avoid negative publicity. For them to do otherwise would be to risk their legitimacy, status, or profitability. The magnitude of this risk is related to whether admissions of false advertising are appropriately disseminated and whether news reports of deviance are frequent, prominent, and specific.

We have shown that FTC actions against STP were ineffective as a control mechanism because corrective advertising was directed away from the consumers originally misled. In like manner, ability to control corporate deviance through newspaper coverage of price-fixing was minimized by the behaviors of the newspapers. Therefore, though it seems reasonable to assume that corporations will avoid actions thought likely to generate negative publicity, there is too little negative publicity associated with corporate deviance for publicity to be an effective control, even in important cases.

CONTROL BY FINES

The most frequently used nonpenetrating controls are monetary fines, with nearly all federal regulatory agencies authorized to impose fines.[34] The Securities and Exchange Commission, for example, is charged with protecting owners and can fine corporations up to $10,-000. The Occupational Safety and Health Administration, charged with safeguarding the safety and health of employees, likewise can levy fines up to $10,000. The Food and Drug Administration protects consumers and is authorized to fine $1,000 for a first offense and $10,000 for each offense thereafter. And the Environmental Protection Agency protects the public-at-large and can fine $25,000 for the first offending day and $50,000 per subsequent offending day.

Additionally, corporations are subject to criminal fines and private damage payments. The Sherman Antitrust Act, for example, now makes price-fixing a felony with a maximum corporate fine of $1 million. It also authorizes private treble damage suits by victims of price-fixing. In the wake of the 1961 electrical case, General Electric paid over $160 million in treble damages.[35] And, in the wake of the 1976 folding-carton conspirary, the corporations involved paid over $200 million.[36]

Reliance on fines is frequent and has an especially appealing logic. Corporations are profit-making organizations. They, therefore, ought to avoid actions thought likely to add significant costs. Because regulatory, criminal, or private damage payments could have such an effect, corporations should avoid those actions.

However, as with control by beneficiary-choice and by publicity, a number of preconditions must be met for control by fines to be effective. These preconditions include

1. High probability of detection.
2. High probability of conviction.
3. Fines that exceed the profits realized by the illegal actions or at least are significant.

The size of fines determines the impact of detection and conviction. Thus, even if the chances of detection and conviction are high, there would be little reason to avoid deviant actions if fines are small. But if the chances of detection and conviction are low, high fines might still provide a deterrent. Hence, the size of fines is the most important of these preconditions. We now will seek to determine if regulatory and criminal fines and private damage payments are sufficiently large to have an effect on deviant corporations.

Regulatory Fines

In his pioneering analysis of *White-Collar Crime,* Edwin Sutherland examined "rebates" as one type of corporate deviance.[37] Rebates give advantage to particular corporations at the expense of others, as when railroads return part of the freight charges to large shippers while charging smaller shippers full fares. In 1887 the Congress outlawed rebates and authorized the newly created Interstate Commerce Commission to fine corporations guilty of offering rebates. Professor Sutherland examined government efforts to enforce this law and observed:

> In the period 1887–1903, only 79 indictments (for rebating) were returned against all railway and industrial corporations in the United States. The government won seventeen of these suits and fines of $16,376 were imposed. *The gains from rebating were obviously far greater than those penalties.*[38]

146   Corporate Deviance

Marshall B. Clinard's recent research indicates that regulatory fines continue to be too small to have a significant impact. He studied the 1,860 violations committed by the nation's 582 largest corporations during 1975 and 1976. Of these violations, 328 resulted in fines, most of which were regulatory.[39] Table 7.3 summarizes Professor Clinard's findings and shows that over 80 percent of the fines paid by corporations of all sizes were no more than $5,000. Table 7.3 also shows that less than 5 percent of the fines exceeded $50,000.

TABLE 7.3.   Size of Corporation by Amount of Monetary Penalty Against Parent Manufacturing Corporations*

Amount of Monetary Penalty Against Corporation	Total	SIZE OF CORPORATION (Net Sales)		
		Small $300–499 Million	Medium $500–999 Million	Large $1 Billion and Up
Up to $5,000	83.8% (N = 275)	53.8%	68.3%	86.5%
$5,001–10,000	4.3% (14)	0.0	9.1	4.1
$10,001–15,000	0.3% (1)	0.0	0.0	0.3
$15,001–20,000	0.3% (1)	0.0	0.0	0.3
$20,001–25,000	0.9% (3)	0.0	0.0	1.0
$25,001–30,000	0.9% (3)	0.0	0.0	1.0
$30,001–35,000	0.3% (1)	0.0	0.0	0.3
$35,001–40,000	0.3% (1)	0.0	4.5	0.0
$40,001–45,000	0.3% (1)	7.7	0.0	0.0
$45,001–50,000	4.0% (13)	15.4	13.6	2.7
$50,001 and up	4.6% (15)	23.1	4.5	3.8
Total	100.0% (N = 328)	100.0% (13)	100.0% (22)	100.0% (293)

*Source: Marshall B. Clinard, *Illegal Corporate Behavior* (Washington, DC: U.S. Government Printing Office, Stock Number 027–000–00843–7, 1979), p. 143. © 1979 by Marshall B. Clinard. Reprinted by permission.

*Source: Marshall B. Clinard, *Illegal Corporate Behavior* (Washington, DC: U.S. Government Printing Office, Stock Number 027–000–00843–7, 1979), p. 143. © 1979 by Marshall B. Clinard. Reprinted by permission.

To get a sense of how such fines might influence a corporation, it is useful to determine the equivalent fine for a person earning $15,000 per year.[40] A "small" corporation with annual sales of $300 million paying a $5,000 fine is paying the equivalent of 2.4 cents. If that same corporation pays a $50,000 fine, a rare occurrence, it would be paying the equivalent of 24 cents.

Criminal Fines

Two of the largest criminal prosecutors for price-fixing were the 1961 heavy electrical equipment case and 1976 folding-carton case (see Table 7.2). Both involved numerous corporate defendants, and both resulted in criminal fines.

The top half of Table 7.4 shows the 1961 gross revenues and criminal fines paid by the large, nonsubsidiary corporations involved in the electrical conspiracy. General Electric was the biggest "loser," paying $437,500 for its involvement in the twenty separate conspiracies. Westinghouse was a close second, paying $372,500.

Criminal fines of $437,500 and $372,500 certainly seem large, and, to a person making $15,000 per year, they would be staggering. However, Table 7.4 also shows that General Electric had 1961 gross revenues of almost $4.5 billion, so its $437,500 fine was the equivalent of $1.45 for our hypothetical individual. Westinghouse's gross revenues were almost $2 billion, making its $372,500 criminal fine equivalent to $2.85. Furthermore, the criminal fines fell far short of the millions of dollars of illegal profits made during the twenty or more years that the conspiracy existed.[41]

The bottom half of Table 7.4 presents comparable data for the 1976 folding-carton case. It shows that criminal fines paid by large, nonsubsidiary corporations were even less significant than in the 1961 case. The biggest loser in 1976 was Federal Paper, which paid the equivalent of $1.80 whereas American Can paid the equivalent of 24 cents.

Private Damage Suits

The Sherman Antitrust Act also provides for private treble damage suits. Victims are entitled to seek triple damage compensation from corporations known to have been involved in price-fixing. In the wake of the 1961 case, for example, General Electric was sued by 1,800 claimants. By June of 1964, 90 percent of these claims had been settled for $160 million. General Electric's gross revenues for 1964, however, were $5.1 billion,[42] making its $160 million payment the equivalent of a one-time expense of $473.27 for a person grossing $15,000 per year.

TABLE 7.4.   Large, Nonsubsidiary Corporations Involved in 1961 and 1976 Price-Fixing Cases

CORPORATION	GROSS REVENUES[b]	CRIMINAL FINE[c]	EQUIVALENT FOR INDIVIDUAL EARNING $15,000[d]
1961 Defendants[a]			
Allis-Chalmers	$ 502,200,000	$127,500	$ 3.75
Carrier	266,300,000	7,500	0.42
Cutler-Hammer	118,300,000	45,000	5.70
Federal Pacific	88,200,000	65,000	10.95
Foster Wheeler	197,900,000	20,000	1.50
General Electric	4,456,800,000	437,500	1.47
I-T-E	111,500,000	92,500	12.30
Ingersoll Rand	181,400,000	20,000	1.65
McGraw-Edison	329,200,000	70,000	3.15
Square D	115,300,000	75,000	9.75
Wagner Electric	65,900,000	10,000	2.25
Westinghouse	1,913,800,000	372,500	2.85
Worthington	189,000,000	20,000	1.50
1976 Defendants[e]			
American Can	3,142,500,000	50,000	0.24
Champion International	2,910,500,000	50,000	0.26
Diamond International	887,100,000	50,000	0.84
Federal Paper	393,600,000	50,000	1.80
International Paper	3,540,000,000	50,000	0.21
Mead	1,599,300,000	50,000	0.47
Potlatch	624,100,000	50,000	1.20
St. Regis	1,642,100,000	50,000	0.45
Weyerhauser	2,868,400,000	50,000	0.26

[a] 1961 nonsubsidiary defendants are those defendants listed separately in *Moody's Handbook of Common Stocks, Fourth Quarter* (New York: Moody's Investors, 1966).
[b] As listed in *Moody's Handbook*.
[c] 1961 data reported in *The New York Times*, 7 February 1961, p. 26 and 2 February 1961; 1976 data reported in "Notice of Hearing on Proposed Class Action Settlements and Proposed Plan of Distribution" In Re Folding Carton Antitrust Litigation, U.S. District Court, Northern District of Illinois, Eastern Division, MDL 250, July 26, 1979.
[d] To determine equivalent for individual earning $15,000, we first divided the criminal fine by 1961 gross revenues. The resulting figure was then multiplied by $15,000. For example, Allis-Chalmers was fined $127,500 and had gross revenues of $502,200,000; $127,500 divided by $502,200,000 equals .00025. and .00025 times $15,000 equals $3.75, the equivalent for an individual earning $15,000.
[e] 1976 nonsubsidiary defendants are those defendants listed separately in *Moody's Handbook of Common Stocks: Winter 1979–80 Edition* (New York: Moody's Investors Services, 1980).

Table 7.5 presents comparable data for the large, nonsubsidiary corporations involved in the 1976 folding-carton conspiracy. By July of 1979 the corporations involved had settled with most plaintiffs for slightly over $200 million. International Paper paid $27 million, the largest proportion of the settlement. However, it had 1978 gross revenues of $4.2 billion, making its payment the equivalent of $96.00. The remaining corporations paid settlements ranging from $20 million to $6.9 million, with equivalents ranging from $675.00 to $36.00.

TABLE 7.5.   Large, Nonsubsidiary[a] Corporations Involved in the 1976 Folding-Carton Industry Price-Fixing Conspiracy, by 1978 Gross Revenues,[b] 1979 Class-Action Treble Damage Settlement,[c] and Equivalent for Individual Earning $15,000[d]

CORPORATION	1978 GROSS REVENUES	1979 CLASS-ACTION TREBLE DAMAGE SETTLEMENT	EQUIVALENT FOR INDIVIDUAL EARNING $15,000
American Can	$3,981,000,000	$15,360,000	$ 57.87
Champion International	3,475,100,000	20,000,000	85.50
Diamond International	1,100,000,000	10,206,000	138.00
Federal Paper	375,600,000	17,068,177	675.00
International Paper	4,200,000,000	27,000,000	96.00
Mead	2,322,100,000	13,414,685	85.50
Potlatch	787,000,000	7,750,000	147.00
St. Regis	2,300,200,000	6,900,000	43.50
Weyerhauser	3,799,400,000	9,469,400	36.00

[a]As indicated by being listed separately in *Moody's Handbook of Common Stocks: Winter 1979–80 Edition* (New York: Moody's Investors Services, 1980).
[b]As listed in *Moody's Handbook.*
[c]In Re Folding Carton Antitrust Litigation, United States District Court, Northern District of Illinois, Eastern Division (MDL 250), July 26, 1979, p. 2.
[d]To determine equivalent for individual earning $15,000, we first divided the 1979 class-action treble damage settlement by 1978 gross revenues. The resulting figure was then multiplied by $15,000. For example, American Can's portion of the class action settlement was $15,360,000, and in 1978 American Can's gross revenues were $3,981,000,000; $15,360,000 divided by $3,981,000,000 equals .0038. And .0038 multiplied by $15,000 equals $57.87, the equivalent for an individual earning $15,000.

Evaluating Control by Fines

The evidence we have considered suggests that an important precondition for the effectiveness of fines largely goes unmet. Regulatory, criminal, and private damage fines all fail to be sufficient. They probably do not usually exceed the profits gained by the actions for which a corporation was fined. It is, therefore, unlikely that fines control corporate deviance.

SUMMARY

Nonpenetrating controls seek to structure environments so that violators will change their actions in the future and potential violators will remain conforming. These controls come in several varieties. In this chapter we examined three of the most important: beneficiary-choice systems, control by publicity, and control by fines.

Each of these controls might be effective when important preconditions are met. Beneficiary-choice systems, for example, are possibly effective to the extent consumers or employees are able to exercise available choices. Publicity is possibly effective to the extent that news reports frequently and prominently link specific corporations with particular episodes. And fines are possibly effective to the extent that they are significant or exceed illegal profits.

However, review of the available evidence indicates that these important preconditions usually are unmet. Consumers and employees fail or are unable to exercise available choices. News reports of corporate deviance are neither frequent nor prominent. And fines fall far short of being sufficient. It therefore seems unlikely that nonpenetrating mechanisms have controlled much corporate deviance.

ANNOTATED SELECTED READINGS

Clinard, Marshall B. *Illegal Corporate Behavior.* Washington, DC: U.S. Government Printing Office, October 1979. Chapter 12 describes alternative strategies for controlling corporate crime.

Galbraith, John Kenneth. *The New Industrial State.* Boston: Houghton Mifflin, 1967. Explains how and why economic realities prevent free markets from working.

Kolko, Gabriel. *The Triumph of Conservatism: A Reinterpretation of American History,* 1900–1916. New York: Free Press, 1963. Describes political processes and individual behaviors that prevented free markets and encouraged concentration and monopoly.

Rourke, Francis E. "Government Regulation through Publicity." In Francis E. Rourke, *Secrecy and Publicity: Dilemmas of Democracy,* Chapter 6. Baltimore: Johns Hopkins Press, 1961. Discusses the power of publicity as a tool by which government can regulate corporate and other behaviors.

Stevenson, Russell B., Jr. "The SEC and the New Disclosure." *Cornell Law Review* 62 (November 1976): 50–91. Discusses the role of the Securities and Exchange Commission as a champion of public disclosure.

Stone, Christopher D. *Where the Law Ends: The Social Control of Corporate Behavior.* New York: Harper & Row, 1975. Analyzes problems and alternatives for controlling corporate behaviors.

NOTES

1. Albert O. Hirschman, *Exit, Voice, and Loyalty* (Cambridge, MA: Harvard U.P., 1970), p. 1.
2. See Ronald L. Soble and Robert E. Dallos, *The Impossible Dream: The Equity Funding Story* (New York: Putnam's, 1974). Also see Chapter 3 of this book.
3. See Paul Brodeur, *Expendable Americans* (New York: Viking, 1974). Also see Chapter 4 of this book.
4. See Gilbert Geis, "White-Collar Crime: The Heavy Electrical Equipment Antitrust Cases of 1961," in M. David Ermann and Richard J. Lundman, eds., *Corporate and Governmental Deviance* (New York: Oxford U.P., 1978), pp. 59–79. Also see Chapter 5 of this book.
5. See John Brooks, "The Bagman," in Rosabeth Moss Kanter and Barry A. Stein, eds., *Life in Organizations: Workplaces as People Experience Them* (New York: Basic Books, 1979), pp. 363–372. Also see Chapter 6 of this book.
6. Other nonpenetrating controls also are quite important. Tax policies in the United States are used to stimulate investment and encourage hiring of unemployed and minority workers. Public utility regulation is used to regulate rates and services of phone, electric, and other "natural monopolies." Some observers advocate "social audits" by which companies would report their social performance much as they now report their financial performance. In Europe corporations have a separate body of laws that are different from laws applied to individuals. We believe, however, that this chapter focuses on the most important nonpenetrating controls.
7. The outstanding academic spokesperson for this approach is Milton Friedman. See, for example, *Free to Choose, A Personal Statement by Milton and Rose Friedman* (New York: Harcourt, 1980). A large corporation

recently sent an unsolicited brochure with Friedman's work to one of the authors. Other corporations sponsor university chairs and public celebrations of this mechanism.

8. Edwin H. Sutherland, *White-Collar Crime* (New York: Holt, Rinehart and Winston, 1949), especially pp. 56–88.

9. Marshall B. Clinard, *Illegal Corporate Behavior* (Washington, DC: U.S. Government Printing Office, 1979), p. 184.

10. See Max Boas and Steve Chain, *Big Mac: The Unauthorized Story of McDonald's* (New York: Dutton, 1976).

11. Lawrence H. Seltzer, *A Financial History of the American Automobile Industry* (Boston: Houghton Mifflin, 1928), p. 19.

12. Ibid., p. 87.

13. *Standard & Poor's Industry Surveys* (New York: Standard and Poor's Corporation, 1977), p. A156.

14. European and Japanese firms partly filled the newcomer role for American car buyers. When domestic companies failed to produce economical cars, large sales of foreign cars that met many buyers' needs prodded American producers to build comparable cars.

15. Paul Eddy, Elaine Potter, and Bruce Page, *Destination Disaster: From the Tri-Motor to the DC–10* (New York: The New York Times Book Company, 1976); Moira Johnston, *The Last Nine Minutes: The Story of Flight 981* (New York: Morrow, 1976).

16. *New York Times,* 26 May 1979, p. 1, "Worst Air Disaster in U.S. History."

17. Brodeur, *Expendable Americans,* pp. 11, 48, and 85. Also see Chapter 4 of this book.

18. David Bolton, *The Grease Machine: The Inside Story of Lockheed's Dollar Diplomacy* (New York: Harper & Row, 1978), pp. 225–252.

19. For a discussion, see M. David Ermann, "The Operative Goals of Corporate Philanthropy," *Social Problems* 25 (June 1978): 504–514.

20. See Clinard, *Illegal,* pp. 29–40.

21. Ibid., p. 222.

22. Other preconditions besides those studied in the following pages also are important. For example, actual or threatened publicity may be most effective when (a) subjects are dependent on public opinion, (b) subjects value being in good public repute, (c) great public odium is attached to the publicized deviance, and (d) the prestige of the agency administering a publicized sanction is greater than the prestige of the subject. See Francis E. Rourke, in *Secrecy and Publicity: Dilemmas of Democracy,* Chapter 6, "Government Regulation through Publicity" (Baltimore: Johns Hopkins Press, 1961).

23. Gilbert Geis, "Deterring Corporate Crime," in Ermann and Lundman, *Corporate and Governmental Deviance,* pp. 282–290.

24. Discussion of the FTC is based upon Clinard, *Illegal,* pp. 29–40.

25. Data are from U.S. District Court, Southern District of New York, *United States of America, Plaintiff* v. *STP Corporation, Defendant, Complaint for Civil Penalties and Injunctive Relief* 78 Civ., *Consent Judgment* 78 Civ.,

United States of America Before the Federal Trade Commission, "In the Matter of STP Corporation and Stern, Walters & Simmons, Inc.," Docket No. C–2777, decision and order. Quote is from p. 203.

26. Art Buchwald, "You Mean We Were Supposed to Tell the Truth?" *Washington Post,* Section F, 19 February 1978, p. 2.

27. "When the Story Broke," *The New Republic* 144 (February 20, 1961): 7; Alan Dershowitz, "Newspaper Publicity and the Electrical Conspiracy," *Yale Law Journal* 71 (December 1961): 288–289; Sandra Evans and Richard J. Lundman, "Newspaper Coverage of Corporate Crime," paper presented at the annual meeting of the American Sociological Association, New York, August 1980.

28. Geis, "The Heavy Electrical," p. 59.

29. The indicted corporations were Allen-Bradley Company, Allis-Chalmers Manufacturing Company, Carrier Corporation, A. B. Chance Company, Clark Controller Company, Cornell-Dubilier Electric Corporation, Cutler-Hammond, Federal Pacific Electric Company, Foster Wheeler Corporation, General Electric, Hubbard & Company, I-T-E Circuit Breaker Company, Ingersoll-Rand Company, Joslyn Manufacturing and Supply Company, Kuhlman Electric Company, Lapp Insulator Company, McGraw-Edison Company, Moloney Electric Company, Ohio Brass Company, H. K. Porter Company, Porcelain Insulator Corporation, Sangamo Electric Company, Schwager-Wood Corporation, Southern States Equipment Corporation, Square D Company, Wagner Electric Corporation, Westinghouse Electric Corporation, C. H. Wheeler Manufacturing Company, and Worthington Corporation.

30. D. Bruce Pearson, *Competitive Impact Statement, United States of America* v. *Alton Box Board Company et al.,* United States District Court, Northern District of Illinois, Eastern Division, Civil Action No. 76 C 597, June 28, 1979, p. 7. The indicted corporations in 1976 were Alton Box Board Company, American Can Company, Brown Company, F. N. Burt Company, Consolidated Packaging Corporation, Diamond International Corporation, Federal Paper Board Company, The A. L. Garber Company, International Paper Company, Burd & Fletcher Company, Champion International Corporation, Container Corporation of America, Eastex Packaging, Fibreboard Corporation, Hoerner Waldorf Corporation, Interstate Folding Box Company, The Mead Corporation, Potlatch Corporation, St. Regis Paper Company, Packaging Corporation of America, Rexham Corporation, and Weyerhauser Company.

31. "When the Story," p. 7.

32. Dershowitz, "Newspaper Publicity," p. 289.

33. Based upon Evans and Lundman, "Newspaper Coverage."

34. Discussion of federal regulatory agencies is based upon Clinard, *Illegal,* pp. 29–40.

35. Geis, "The Heavy Electrical," p. 64.

36. "Notice of Hearing on Proposed Class Action Settlements and Proposed Plan of Distribution," *In Re Folding Carton Antitrust Litigation,* United

States District Court, Northern District of Illinois, Eastern Division, MDL 250, July 26, 1979, p. 2. It should be noted that several plaintiffs did not participate in the class-action settlement. They are pursuing individual suits with awards expected after this book goes to print. It is reasonable to expect that these awards will increase the $200 million class-action figures.

37. Sutherland, *White-Collar Crime,* pp. 89–94.
38. Ibid., p. 90.
39. Clinard, *Illegal,* p. 143, included an unknown number of criminal fines in his data.
40. This and later calculations of the equivalent for a person earning $15,000 per year were inspired by Geis, who observed that General Electric's criminal fine in the 1961 case "was no more unsettling than a $3 parking fine would be to a man with an income of $175,000 a year." See Geis, "The Heavy Electrical," p. 63.

    We have chosen to use gross corporate revenues for this and later comparisons because of the availability of consistent data. More importantly, fines seem more reasonably considered as an expense of doing business than as an independent deduction from profits. A comparison of fines to profits would exaggerate the impact of the penalty, for the pattern of deviant acts in most cases probably produced added profits far greater than the cost of the fine.
41. Richard Austin Smith, "The Incredible Electrical Conspiracy," *Fortune* (April 1961): 132.
42. Geis, "The Heavy Electrical," p. 64.

Penetrating controls

A consent decree settling numerous charges of discrimination against women and racial minorities directed the Bell companies to establish compliance officers whose duties were spelled out in detail. The current regulations of the Food and Drug Administration require the drug companies to establish quality-control units, many of whose powers and obligations are prescribed by the government.... [A]t least one federal judge has warned a recidivist corporate polluter that if it did not mend its ways, the court would send its own designate into the company—as a sort of inhouse "probation officer"—to take over the pollution-control activities of corporate officers who might be interfering with the process of rehabilitation.

—*Christopher Stone*[1]

The "recidivist corporate polluter" cited by Stone on the preceding page was ARCO, a major oil company, charged with spilling oil into a Chicago canal. The standard *non* penetrating control was a sixty-five-year-old law permitting a maximum fine of $2,500. ARCO pleaded no contest and appeared quite willing to pay the fine. In the preceding year, it had total revenues of $3.3 billion,[2] making $2,500 the equivalent of one cent for an individual earning $15,000 per year.

However, the same leaky plant previously had been convicted of the same violation. The judge, therefore, decided to give the company forty-five days to complete a program to handle oil spillage. If not successful within the time specified, ARCO would be put on probation with its own probation officer placed in the corporation to oversee needed changes personally. The problem was solved before forty-five days.[3]

The ARCO case and others like it[4] are unusual. Conventional wisdom still holds that government and other outsiders must not penetrate corporations. It argues that "interference" in internal corporate affairs is undesirable, perhaps even immoral. In the words of John Kenneth Galbraith:

> The corporate charter . . . accords the corporation a large area of independent action in the conduct of its affairs. And this freedom is defended as a sacred right. Nothing in American business attitudes is so iniquitous as government interference in the internal affairs of the corporation. The safeguards here, both in law and custom, are great.[5]

Recently, however, there have been changes. A relatively large number of people have advocated penetration of corporate boundaries for purposes of control. Although their proposals vary, these people share an increasing willingness to penetrate boundaries in an effort to control corporate deviance.

Preview of the Chapter

This chapter describes and evaluates three of the most important examples of penetraing controls. The controls we will discuss try to change corporate chartering, protect "whistle-blowers," and punish executives involved in corporate criminality.

CHANGING CORPORATE CHARTERS

The government document that formalizes creation of an organization is its "charter." Every organization—whether business, labor union, hospital, or university—has a charter that requires it to perform certain activities, permits it to perform others, and prohibits still others. The goal of the organization may be trading with the East Indies, producing automobiles, or providing telephone services. In all cases, the corporate charter creates the organization as an entity and specifies what it can or cannot do.

Ralph Nader,[6] among others,[7] believes that change of corporate chartering is one way to control corporations. He argues that existing charters give corporations more autonomy and flexibility than historically intended or currently warranted. He, therefore, proposes restrictive federal chartering of corporations. To understand Mr. Nader's argument and proposals requires first understanding the history of corporate chartering.

History of Corporate Chartering[8]

Charters originally were quite restrictive. They frequently specified distribution of profits, voting rights of shareholders, decisions that could be made by managers, location of corporate operations, and number of years the corporation could exist. They also specified corporate purposes and activities and prohibited expansion into unspecified areas. For instance, a group chartered to weave cotton could not start growing cotton or farming silkworms unless it first changed its charter. Such charter restrictions were intended to control incorporating groups and prevent growth of undesirable social power.

Charters were issued by individual states. In the state where a corporation sought to incorporate, its application would be carefully reviewed to ensure its positive contribution to the public welfare. This procedure gave each state

> a chance to consider each particular application on its merit, and to tailor the company-to-be's powers and privileges, and even its size and debt structure, to the limits appropriate to its particular undertaking. When, for example, Massachusetts granted the Maine Flour Mills a charter in 1818, it limited the total property the corporation might hold to $50,000, of which the land could not exceed $30,000 in value and had—all of it—to be in Kennebec County.[9]

In the early 1800s, state legislatures loosened some of these restrictions in order to improve commerce, remove political involvement, and reduce the legislative burden. They abandoned the requirement that notice and subsequent public discussion occur before each proposed charter could be granted. They no longer considered public consequences of a proposed incorporation to be grounds for granting or denying it. Any "lawful" business chartered in Connecticut after 1837 could file a standard document with the state, pay an incorporation tax, and be granted a charter. As the process was simplified, controls inevitably were weakened.

However, incorporation procedures instituted by Connecticut and other states between the turn of the century and 1860 still were highly restrictive by today's standards. Review of them reveals many restrictions no longer in effect:

> First, there were limitations upon authorized capital. Well into the nineteenth century, few states permitted corporations to aggregate more than $500,000 or $1,000,000. Similarly, severe limitations were imposed on the amount of indebtedness, and the power of one corporation to hold stock in another was neither conferred nor implied. Second, limitations upon the scope of a business corporation's powers were also universal. Until 1837 every state in the Union limited incorporation to a single purpose or a limited number of purposes, such as a particular transportation, mining, or manufacturing project. Third, corporate charters were limited to a term of years—generally, 20, 30, or 50 years in duration. And corporations were limited geographically as well.[10]

Competition Between States

Such limitations began to disappear in the late 1800s because states started to compete for incorporation fees. In the 1890s, New Jersey gave corporations complete control over their life span and their geographical locations, as well as the right to merge or consolidate in any manner they might choose. At the same time it removed all limits on their size and market concentration. And it reduced its protection of shareholder powers when it stopped specifying conditions under which corporate bylaws could be changed.

New Jersey's liberalization was carried still further by Delaware. The Delaware Act of 1898 contained an important provision: assuming it was not contrary to state law, a corporate charter could contain any provision incorporators might choose to insert. Incorporators thus were given great latitude, with control of the corporation by the state essentially abandoned.

By 1912 most states permitted perpetual charters and had liberal merger and consolidation rules. Virtually all permitted the organization of a corporation for "any lawful purpose" as they raced to make their jurisdictions the most tempting to would-be incorporators. Thus, General Motors' charter, drawn up in 1916, could broadly list its purposes to cover manufacturing, buying, selling, and dealing in all sorts of motor vehicles and their component parts, engaging in all conceivable stock dealings, manufacturing of any sort, and business and property dealings which "the corporation may deem proper and convenient" to further its interest. The charter also was not limited by geography, size, or time.

However, the race was not yet over. In 1963, Delaware moved to solidify its position as the best place for management to incorporate. A committee was formed to survey the increasingly loose statutes of other states, solicit persons serving current or potential incorporators, and then recommend amending or replacing the existing law. The preamble to the bill establishing the committee states in admirably candid terms the goals of the legislature:

> *WHEREAS,* the State of Delaware has a long and beneficial history as the domicile of nationally known corporations; and
> *WHEREAS,* the favorable climate which the State of Delaware has traditionally provided for corporations has been a leading source of revenue for the State; and
> *WHEREAS,* many States have enacted new corporation laws in recent years in an effort to compete with Delaware for corporate business; and
> *WHEREAS,* there has been no comprehensive revision of the Delaware Corporation Law since its enactment in 1898; and
> *WHEREAS,* the General Assembly of the State of Delaware declares it to be the public policy of the State to maintain a favorable business climate and to encourage corporations to make Delaware their domicile . . .[11]

The legislation that emerged retained much existing law, thereby keeping precedents set through many years of Delaware judicial decisions. The state was to be sold to incorporators on the grounds of its stability and its legal system known for a long history of consistently pro-management decisions. Some changes were made to reduce further the rights of shareholders. Other changes permitted corporations to "establish and carry out pension, profit-sharing, stock option, stock purchase, stock bonus, retirement, benefit incentive, and compensation plans, trusts and provision—for any and all of its directors, officers or employees. . . . "[12] Loans to officers and employees could be authorized by the board of directors without collateral or interest or disclosure to other stockholders. And corporations were empowered to pay for costs incurred during lawsuits brought against corporate officers, employees, or agents.

Delaware's willingness to abandon all aspects of chartering except fee collection has had its intended effects. The state is "home" for half of the nation's 500 largest industrial firms. In 1979 it realized $64,-000,000 in revenues from corporate chartering. Other states, of course, have attempted to gain some of this revenue in a continuing competition sometimes labeled "a race for the bottom."

Ralph Nader's Proposed Reforms

Given this history of state chartering, it now is possible to evaluate Ralph Nader's proposal for restrictive federal chartering. Individual states understandably have failed to control corporations. Tighter controls by any state acting alone would merely mean few incorporations and little revenue for it. Thus, if Delaware were to reform its laws, corporations simply would move to less restrictive states. This would leave the Delaware treasury poorer, but its former corporations as free as ever from social control. Hence, charter reform cannot occur as long as states compete for the revenue that corporate executives direct to whatever state has the least restrictive chartering.

Mr. Nader's proposals, therefore, begin with a single federal chartering system for large corporations.[13] This would eliminate opportunities for corporate giants to play states against one another in order to get continually weaker controls. However, it does not end with a change in the issuer of charters. It also views chartering as a way to change corporations in order to bring greater advantages to normative beneficiaries.

For owners, federal chartering would change the current situation in which most members of corporate boards of directors are actually part-time agents of corporate management. Mr. Nader proposes full-time individuals capable of representing shareholders. Board members would have staffs and specific mechanisms by which they and their staffs could collect internal information. They also would review important business decisions, set salary scales, and select key personnel. Shareholders themselves would have more influence because they would get more and clearer information, democratically elect board members, review important corporate decisions, and more effectively bring legal action when their wishes are not met.

Employees, too, would have representation on the board, with one director specifically charged with "employee welfare." This director would collect detailed information about corporate activities that affect employees, particularly dangers in the workplace and patterns of minority employment. And corporations would be "constitutionalized," giving employees the rights on the job that they enjoy elsewhere as citizens: rights of free speech, assembly, and privacy. Prohibited would be widespread practices of pre-employment lie detector tests, spying on current employees, maintaining inaccessible or unchallengeable personnel files, and "unjust dismissals of whistle blowers and others."

The customers in the Nader proposal would be protected by creating many competitive firms out of the very small number that now dominate most industries. Corporations with monopoly or semimonopoly power would be divided up, whereas those seeking such power in the future would be prohibited through clearly specified mechanisms and criteria. In addition, advertisement regulations would be instituted, and consumers would be able to have more ready access to the courts. And, as with the other normative beneficiaries, consumers would have their member of the board of directors charged with "consumer protection."

For the public-at-large, finally, Mr. Nader's proposal would provide additional disclosure of corporate activities. In each case of pollution, for instance, the corporation would have to identify plants involved, materials discharged, applicable regulations, corporate violations of those regulations, and resulting lawsuits and other actions. In each major plant relocation, the corporation would be required to issue "community impact statements" before a move could be made. And, finally, a member of the board of directors responsible for "environmental protection and community relations" would represent the public-at-large.

Another Proposed Reform

Christopher Stone, in his influential book *Where the Law Ends,* [14] also has called for change in boards of directors. Professor Stone proposes creation of two new types of board members. The first, general public directors (GPDs), would be placed in varying numbers in all large corporations. These individuals would be selected and paid by the general public through an appropriate federal commission while maintaining an office at the firm's place of business. Their activities would include making corporate leaders more conscious of social issues, assuring legal compliance, signaling the need for new legislation, and acting as conduits for whistle-blowers within the corporation.

To do this, GPDs would be authorized to hire their own staffs, inspect corporate books, be seated on corporate committees, and deal with a wide variety of personnel matters. Their ultimate goal would be to represent the general public's interest in the ongoing functioning of large and socially important corporations.

A second group of directors called special public directors (SPDs) would have functions similar to general public directors except that their attention would be focused on a problem. They would be placed in corporations only when specific violations made such dramatic actions compelling. One example Professor Stone considers is the problem of asbestos discussed in Chapter 4. In such a case, as in cases of pollution, consumer safety, or nuclear energy, an appropriately skilled SPD would be appointed. He points out that this already is done to protect corporate shareholders when a corporation is placed in bankruptcy, but it is not done to protect consumers or persons living in the neighborhood of a toxic plant.

Evaluating Charter Reform

Charter reform is being advocated by Ralph Nader to control corporate activities in a number of areas. However, federal chartering would not be needed to implement his proposals for citizenship rights in the workplace, breaking up of large corporations, or disclosure of pollution. These and most of the other changes he suggests could be implemented by using existing legislative options. Their lack of progress is related to federal legislative realities rather than to state chartering.

However, federal chartering might be necessary to get the systematic changes in boards of directors advocated by Mr. Nader and by Christopher Stone. These changes would be difficult to implement under present state chartering arrangements. And they appear at first glance to be possibly effective. However, they have two major problems.

First, actual attempts to change boards have been disappointing. A stockholder suit against Phillips Petroleum, for example, resulted from illegal campaign contributions by Phillips to Richard Nixon's re-election campaign. In settling this suit, management agreed that the board of directors, which overwhelmingly had been composed of Phillips executives, be reconstituted to make at least 60 percent of its members nonemployees. Phillips also agreed to place outside directors in control of key committees of the board. The reconstituted board is held responsible for preventing illegal contributions and representing shareholder interests. However, this and similar attempts to restructure the board of directors have had poor results because new directors are drawn from the same basic pool as previous ones and because newly structured boards do not act in notably different ways.[15]

Second, even a successfully restructured board would have only limited influence on its corporation. Power in large corporations rests in the hands of no single person or even in small groups of individuals known as "directors." Instead, power rests in the organization itself[16] with day-to-day operations under the control of "a small army of technocrats."[17] Most important decisions are, and often must be, made routinely by committees of technical specialists many levels below the board. Experience to date, therefore, suggests that use of chartering to require beneficiary representation on boards of directors and similar changes is not likely to provide substantial protection against deviance.

PROTECTING WHISTLE-BLOWERS[18]

Whistle-blowing refers to actions taken by organizational members to alert outsiders to deviance. Whistle-blowers believe their organizations are involved in illegal, inefficient, or immoral activities. They inform regulators, journalists, or other outsiders about their beliefs and thereby expose their organizations to possible public scrutiny and sanction.

Defective, dangerous, and polluting machines and motor vehicles were publicized initially by whistle-blowers, as were unsafe airplanes and toys, illegal corporate contributions, and many Watergate-related activities. Despite its effectiveness in these and a few other cases, however, whistle-blowing cannot now be considered a widely used or important control mechanism.

Many observers argue that whistle-blowing is infrequent because whistle-blowers run considerable risks. They therefore advocate protection of such individuals from the personal costs of dissent. In order to evaluate their proposals, we must first understand the costs associated with whistle-blowing.

Personal Costs of Whistle-Blowing

The experiences of Charles Pettis and Ernie Fitzgerald graphically illustrate the personal costs of whistle-blowing. Charles Pettis was an engineer hired to oversee construction of a road across the Andes in Peru.[19] His firm had been hired by the Peruvian government to protect Peruvian interests by enforcing contract specifications.

After reviewing the road design, Mr. Pettis became convinced that the construction plans needed complete reworking. The road was to be cut through deep channels in mountains highly susceptible to slides. He feared costs in both human lives and slide removal, and he was correct. When thirty-one men were killed during a serious slide, he refused to charge the Peruvian government for the extra cost or assure them of the safety of the design.

At first his own company supported him, but its attitude changed after high-level contacts with the construction firm that stood to lose significantly by his decision. The two firms often worked together and were interdependent, but Mr. Pettis would not change. For his lack of loyalty, he and his family were subjected to great psychological pressure. His children had eggs thrown at them, and he was considered a traitor by members of his own firm. Ultimately, he was fired, and he reported that he was blackballed in the rest of the construction industry. Blackballing usually is informal and not documentable but, a federal government investigation concluded, "The fact remains . . . that he has applied for thirty-one jobs [in two years] and has been unsuccessful in gaining employment in [his] field."[20]

The best-known instance of whistle-blowing and its personal cost is the case of Ernie Fitzgerald.[21] Mr. Fitzgerald exposed cost overruns on the Lockheed C–5A Air Force plane. By pointing out a $2 billion over-run, he started a long debate questioning the company's efficiency and affecting its solvency. In so doing, he also incurred more than $400,000 in legal fees in a fight to regain his Defense Department job.

Mr. Fitzgerald was hired in 1965 by the Air Force as a deputy for management and assigned to cost control problems in many large weapons systems. Frustrated after fruitless attempts to cut waste, he agreed to testify before a congressional committee in 1968. As a result of that testimony he was removed from his regular duties and assigned to analyzing cost problems of bowling alleys in Thailand. He was no longer invited to attend even routine management meetings and was accused of everything from being a penny pincher to being both a womanizer and gay. Ultimately, he was dismissed from his job as a direct result of his whistle-blowing, although later the Air Force was made to reinstate him. However, his awesome legal costs were not reimbursed. In May 1977 it was ruled that being made whole again for whistle-blowing does not include recovery of legal costs.

Both of these whistle-blowers experienced heavy personal costs, and their losses probably are typical. Loss of income, job security, and reputation as well as loss of colleagueship and even friendship are the very real costs of whistle-blowing. It is because the personal costs of whistle-blowing are so high that proposals have been advanced to protect whistle-blowers.

Proposed Reforms

Some protections for whistle-blowers already exist. Eight public laws now contain "employee protection" sections.[22] These laws[23] allow appeals to the secretary of labor by employees fired or otherwise harassed for reporting corporate violations. The secretary must investigate complaints and may hold formal hearings. An employee whose complaint is upheld may receive reinstatment, back wages, and possibly reimbursement of attorney's fees.

One suggested reform is to guarantee to reimburse attorney's fees when a whistle-blowing employee wins in court. Had such a policy been in effect for Ernie Fitzgerald, his $400,000 in legal fees would have been paid by the Air Force. Another proposal is to create an agency of lawyers and researchers to defend government employees facing reprisals for their whistle-blowing. This proposal could readily be adapted to the needs of corporate employees, with funds collected by a payroll checkoff system familiar to most employees. Also, there have been suggestions that more corporations institute programs whereby employees with social concerns may directly air their concerns to a corporate ombudsman.[24]. This would bypass the normal censoring of bad news as it flows upward through corporate channels.

Additional ideas come from other countries. In the Soviet Union, for example, whistle-blowing long has been encouraged.[25] One means is the press, using letters to the editor. These letters are important ways to propose changes publicly and to criticize individuals and units that are lagging. They provide a kind of open season on bureaucrats. So long as they are careful to select targets not too high in the power hierarchy and to avoid any appearance of criticizing the regime or basic Communist Party policy, Soviet citizens may through these letters vent rather strongly worded complaints against the work of the government bureaucracy in such matters as supplying consumers' goods and repairing and maintaining housing and public facilities.[26] Writers ordinarily are safe from reprisal if their attacks are on relatively minor officials and do not question basic institutions.

Evaluating Proposed Reforms

Protection of whistle-blowers from the personal costs of their dissent rests upon the simple assumption that organizational members fail to whistle-blow because they fear harassment. In order to evaluate the likely effectiveness of proposed reforms, therefore, we must determine the extent that fear of reprisal is a major obstacle to whistle-blowing. Review of the available evidence suggests that other factors also constrain whistle-blowing and must be considered, with loyalty perhaps the most important.

Whistle-blowing is limited by the loyalty of individuals to their organizations.[27] Many people take great pride in organizational membership and place great emphasis on cooperation and team play. They therefore dislike actions such as whistle-blowing that suggest disloyalty. This is partly because they are encouraged and rewarded for loyalty and believe disloyalty is wrong. Consider the claim by James Roche, former head of General Motors, that

some critics are now busy eroding another support of free enterprise—the loyalty of a management team, with its unifying values of cooperative work. Some of the enemies of business now encourage an employee to be disloyal to the enterprise. They want to create suspicion and disharmony, and pry into the proprietary interests of the business. However this is labelled—industrial espionage, whistle blowing, or professional responsibility—it is another tactic for spreading disunity and creating conflict.[28]

Mr. Roche is appealing to our general distrust of tattletales, stool pigeons, turncoats, and others disloyal to their group. He also is arguing that organizational loyalty in the face of outside pressure is a virtue. Because of such attitudes, many people are loyal to their organizations even when personal penalties for disloyalty are absent.

Why this is the case is puzzling, and many plausible explanations can be offered.[29] But whatever the reason, such loyalty does exist. It serves universities seeking funds from alumni, and it serves nations seeking soldiers for armies. It serves football teams and political parties. Not surprisingly, then, loyalty also serves business organizations whose members that dislike what they observe nevertheless choose not to act. Promises of protection have no impact on such choices.

We, therefore, place only limited confidence in efforts that assume fear of reprisal is the major obstacle to whistle-blowing. Though many people are constrained by fear, many more are constrained by their loyalty. Protection of whistle-blowers does nothing to overcome this important constraint.

IMPOSING INDIVIDUAL PENALTIES

Punishment of individuals involved in corporate crime has been extraordinarily infrequent in the United States. For example, Marshall B. Clinard found that only 1.5 percent of all enforcement efforts in 1975 and 1976 produced conviction of a corporate officer for failure to carry out legal responsibilities in the corporation. And only about one-fifth of the corporate officers charged were at the highest corporate levels.[30] Jail sentences for those convicted of traditional offenses rarely exceeded thirty days, and monetary fines generally have been so low as to be inconsequential.

For instance, in the investigation following Watergate, twenty-one business executives admitted illegally giving politicians corporate funds.[31] Table 8.1 shows that only two served jail sentences; and those, for only a few months. Their fines, mostly one or two thousand dollars, would not have affected their life-styles even if they had been made to pay them because they were not indemnified by their corporations. Most are still with their companies or doing related work—this despite the fact that their illegal activities were premeditated and socially significant.

Proposed and Actual Reforms

There is evidence of a modest trend toward increased personal accountability for corporate executives and directors. In the U.S. House of Representatives, recently proposed legislation to protect employees and consumers provides that a manager responsible for informing employees and federal agencies about dangerous products may be personally fined $50,000 and imprisoned two years for failing to act.[32] Similarly, recently passed legislation intended to prevent corporate personnel from bribing foreign officials contains individual penalties of up to $10,000 and five years imprisonment.[33] Finally, penalties under the Sherman Antitrust Act have been stiffened so that individual violation now is a felony with a maximum fine of $10,000.[34]

The courts have added to this modest trend toward increased personal accountability. The most widely publicized case involved John Park, president of Acme Markets.[35] At the time of the case, Acme was a national retail food chain with 36,000 employees, 874 retail stores, and 16 warehouses. Mr. Park's problems resulted from a warehouse complex in Baltimore. In late 1971, the warehouse was inspected by an investigator from the Food and Drug Administration (FDA). In the basement of the warehouse he "found extensive evidence of rodent infestation in the form of rat and mouse pellets throughout the entire perimeter area and along the wall."[36] In addition, the doors leading to the basement of the warehouse and from the rail sidings had openings through which rodents might enter, and there were rodent pellets on various boxes stored in the warehouse. At a later date he found rat and mouse leavings and nesting materials, live and dead rodents, and liquid drain cleaner stored by cooked ham. The warehouse was extremely overcrowded and had an accumulation of trash.

Following the inspection, an FDA official wrote Mr. Park, informing him of these conditions. The letter was explicit about the problems and observed that they "obviously existed for a long period of time without any detection, or were completely ignored."[37] In response, Mr. Park directed the vice-president in charge of the Baltimore division to write a letter indicating various steps that had been taken to improve the situation. A second inspection was conducted about three months after the first and—though it noted some improvements—still found much evidence of rodent infestation.

One year later, the U.S. government filed suit against the corporation and against Mr. Park for violations in the two inspections. Predictably, the company pleaded guilty to all counts while its president pleaded not guilty and was given a jury trial. The prosecutions' argument essentially was that "Mr. Park was responsible for seeing that

TABLE 8.1. Persons Admitting Making Illegal Corporate Contributions to Politicians, 1973–1974, by Corporation, Punishment, and Current Status

NAME	COMPANY	PUNISHMENT	CURRENT STATUS
George M. Steinbrenner, 3rd	American Ship Building	$15,000	Still chairman at $50,000/yr.
John H. Melcher, Jr.		2,500	Discharged. Practicing law in Cleveland
Orin E. Atkins*	Ashland Oil	$ 1,000	Still chairman at $314,000/yr.
Harold S. Nelson	Associated Milk Producers	4-months prison $10,000	Resigned. Now in commodities exports
David L. Parr		4-months prison $10,000	Resigned.
Stuart H. Russell		2-years prison**	Resigned. Now in private law practice
Harding L. Lawrence	Braniff International	$ 1,000	Still chairman at $335,000/yr.
H. Everett Olson	Carnation	$ 1,000	Still chairman at $212,500/yr.
Ray Dubrowin	Diamond International	$ 1,000	Still V.P. for public affairs
Russell DeYoung	Goodyear Tire & Rubber	$ 1,000	Still chairman of 2 committees at $306,000/yr. Also collecting pension of $144,000/yr.

Claude C. Wild, Jr.	Gulf Oil	$ 1,000	Consultant in Washington, D.C.
Charles N. Huseman	HMS Electric	$ 1,000	Still president
William G. Lyles, Sr.	LBC&W Inc.	$ 2,000	Still chairman
Richard L. Allison	Lehigh Valley Cooperative Farmers	Suspended Fine of $1,000	Discharged
Harry Heltzer	3M	$500	Retired as chairman, but does special projects at $100,000/yr.
Thomas V. Jones	Northrop	$ 5,000	Still chief executive at $286,000/yr.
James Allen		$ 1,000	Retired as V.P. with pension est. at $36,000/yr.
William W. Keeler	Phillips Petroleum	$ 1,000	Retired with pension est. at $201,742/yr.
Harry Ratrie	Ratrie, Robbins & Schweitzer	1-month probation	Still president
Augustus Robbins, 3rd		1-month probation	Still Exec. V.P.
Raymond Abendroth	Time Oil	$ 2,000	Still president

*Pleaded no contest
**Under appeal

Source: Michael C. Jensen, "Watergate Donors Still Riding High," *The New York Times*, Section 3, 24 August 1975, page 1. © 1975 The New York Times Company. Reprinted by permission.

sanitation was taken care of, and he had a system set up that was supposed to do that. This system didn't work three times. At some point, Mr. Park had to be held responsible for the fact that his system isn't working."

Unlike most cases of corporate deviance, Mr. Park did not and could not claim that he was unaware of the problem. He did claim that as president of a large corporation, he had no choice but to delegate responsibility to others and that in this case he had no reason to suspect his subordinates were not complying with federal regulations. He also contended that by acting through subordinates he had done everything a person of his position could do to correct the problem. The jury found him guilty on all five counts, and the judge fined him $250. He appealed that decision and had it reversed by the Court of Appeals, only to have it upheld by the U.S. Supreme Court.

Responses to the Park Case

This case has drawn wide attention because, unlike previous cases, the person found guilty did not have a close supervisory relationship to the violations that occurred. No previous court cases involved senior executives who were remote from, and personally uninvolved in, a violation. The legal system in this case rejected defenses of earlier periods, such as those in the electrical conspiracy, where executives who were uninformed or were able to remain uniformed were not found guilty. But the Park case may be unusual because Mr. Park obviously knew of the problems. He did not claim ignorance of the problems but only ignorance of the failure of corrective action.

The Park case is significant because it suggests that a jury was willing to hold someone somewhere in the corporation responsible for corporate activity. Its impact is not limited to Acme and Mr. Park. In the words of one of the many articles reviewing legal issues in this case, similar future rulings would

> cause significant changes in the organization structures and decision-making processes of corporations that deal in consumer products. . . . The companies . . . must initiate new procedures and develop new safeguards to insure their economic survival and well-being as well as to protect their top executives from exposure to personal liability for good faith efforts made on a company's behalf during the normal course of business.[38]

The business community has been quick to take note of this modest trend towards increased personal accountability for executives. A *Harvard Business Review* article warned that "U.S. corporate officers are increasingly at risk of criminal prosecution either for their companies' failure to comply with federal regulations or for other organizational wrongdoing."[39] And a recent full-page advertisement in the business section of *The New York Times* by the Insurance Company of North America warned corporate directors:

> Individual stockholders and stockholder groups are frequent plaintiffs in actions brought against directors and officers of publicly held companies, both large and small. Employees and former employees, customers, government agencies and prior owners of acquired companies are other potential plaintiffs.[40]

The advertisement went on to note that the Insurance Company of North American could offer "directors' and officers' liability insurance" to those who fear being held personally accountable.

Evaluating Proposed Reforms

In all, there exists evidence of a modest trend toward holding business executives personally accountable for corporate deviance, but the outlook is not promising. Let us begin with what are not the problems with proposed reforms based in these trends. The problem is not public indifference. Citizens frequently appear to be indignant about corporate deviance. Respondents to a 1969 survey reported that a manufacturer of unsafe cars was worse than a mugger (68 percent to 22 percent) and that a price-fixing executive was worse than a burglar (54 percent to 28 percent).[41] A poll conducted for the business community in 1975 revealed that "an increasing proportion—72% of [the] latest survey vs. 65% in 1973—believe that '[executives] do everything they can to make a profit even if it means ignoring the public's needs.' Indeed . . . 50% . . . doubt whether business has any social conscience at all."[42]

The problem also does not appear to be an inability of penalties to prevent individual participation in deviance. Although evidence is limited to specific deterrence,[43] it does suggest that more severe sanctions for individual executives might deter:

> Jail terms have a self-evident deterrent impact upon corporate officials who belong to a social group that is exquisitely sensitive to status deprivation and censure. The white-collar offender and his business colleagues . . . are apt to learn well the lesson intended by a prison term.[44]

What then are the problems?[45] One is that legislators on both the federal and state levels have intimate ties with the world of business. Executives are their friends and supporters. Defrauded shareholders, maimed workers, and price-fixing victims are not. Legislation reflects these patterns of personal relationships.

The second problem is that judges and jurors, like legislators, seem not to share the public's indignation. Jurors often are sympathetic to individual defendants, acquitting individuals while simultaneously convicting corporations. Judges share social class origins and backgrounds with defendants and are reluctant to send them to jail. Despite clear options permitting meaningful penalties for corporate officials, judges regularly impose minor fines and suspended sentences.

Only eleven cases involved jail sentences for businessmen during the first fifty years of the Sherman Antitrust Act (1890–1940). Ten of these contained violence or intimidation rather than typical antitrust violations. From 1940 to 1955 prison sentences were imposed in only eleven cases, but most of them were suspended. It was not until 1959, almost seventy years after the law was passed, that significant use was made of its individual penalties. The two-year flurry that followed had little long-term effect, however, and judges have gone back to their original reluctance to impose jail sentences.[46]

Finally, there are numerous structural problems that compound the attitudinal ones described earlier. Corporate structures make it difficult to determine that a specific policy formulator rather than a lower-level policy implementer was responsible for a violation. Legal procedures permit executives to use "no contest pleas" and "consent decrees," which dramatically reduce chances of penalty. Finally and very importantly, significant corporate acts such as failure to produce a feasible and less polluting engine would not result in legal sanctions against executives.

In all, therefore, we cannot place great hope on a modest trend toward increased personal accountability for corporate executives. It is not that such a trend must prove ineffective. It is that the trend is modest and likely to remain so.

CONCLUSIONS

As the legitimacy of corporations and other large organizations has declined, the perceived inviolability of their shells also has declined. A considerable body of thought holds that corporations, if left to themselves or merely pressured from outside, will not avoid deviance. Hence it is argued that normative beneficiaries and their agents now must penetrate corporations and influence the people who make decisions, change the way their decisions are made, and inform the public about those decisions.

Penetrating controls to protect the rights of some normative benefi-ciaries are not new, however. To protect the rights of beneficiaries with direct financial stakes, companies for many years have been placed in the hands of receivers. In the case of Equity Funding, for example, control of the corporation was transferred to a court-appointed trustee, who reconstituted the corporation to salvage maximum benefit for some of the firm's economic beneficiaries. What is new is the opinion that corporate shells should be penetrated to protect nonfinancial rights of employees, customers, and the public-at-large.

We have analyzed three ways such penetrations can occur, but we have excluded other penetrating controls because we consider them less important. However, exclusion of one must be explained.

Large corporations could be nationalized and thus made formally responsible to the public-at-large. Undoubtedly, nationalization would have many significant social consequences. But to the authors of this book, control of corporate deviance would not be one of those conse-quences.

Nationalized corporations still would be organizations with essen-tially the same goals they currently have. Security, growth, and auton-omy are important goals for *all* organizations. Corporate deviance is the product of organizational patterns that serve these goals. Deviance does not result from avarice by or for powerless shareholders. In fact, government and other nonprofit organizations also routinely are devi-ant.[47]

Unfortunately, too little is known about the social technologies needed to make corporations serve even their current normative bene-ficiaries. Better mechanisms for controlling organizations thus are more necessary than additional but unenforceable corporate obliga-tions.

ANNOTATED SELECTED READINGS

Geis, Gilbert. "Deterring Corporate Crime." In M. David Ermann and Richard J. Lundman, eds., *Corporate and Governmental Deviance*. New York: Oxford U.P., 1978. Pp. 278–296. Advocates penalties for individual corporate execu-tives.

McVisk, William, "Toward a Rational Theory of Criminal Liability for the Corporate Executive." *The Journal of Criminal Law and Criminology* 69:1 (1978):75–91. Studies the legal history and rationale for imposing penalties on individual employees.

Nader, Ralph; Mark Green; and Joel Seligman. *Taming the Giant Corporation.* New York: Norton, 1976. Attacks corporate behavior and advocates federal chartering. Also provides history of state chartering.

Nader, Ralph; Peter J. Petkas; and Kate Blackwell, eds. *Whistle Blowing.* New York: Bantam Books, 1972. Analysis and case histories of persons exposing the illegal or harmful acts of their own organizations.

Seavoy, Ronald E. "The Public Service Origins of The American Business Corporation." *The Business History Review* 52 (Spring 1978): 30–60. Describes the history of corporate creation from English common law to early nineteenth-century America.

Sethi, S. Prakash, and Robert N. Katz. "The Expanding Scope of Personal Criminal Liability of Corporate Executives—Some Implications of *United States* v. *Park.*" *Food Drug Cosmetic Law Journal* (December 1977): 544–570. Provides detailed description and analysis of the Park case.

Solomon, Lewis D. "Restructuring the Corporate Board of Directors; Fond Hope—Faint Promise?" *Michigan Law Review* 76:4 (March 1978): 581–611. Evaluates efforts to restructure corporate boards.

NOTES

1. Christopher Stone, "Controlling Corporate Misconduct," *The Public Interest* 48 (Summer 1977): 63–64.
2. *Standard Corporate Description* (New York: Standard & Poor's Corporation Publishers, 1980), pp. 8770–8771.
3. Ultimately, ARCO successfully challenged the judge's ruling.
4. See Stone, "Controlling."
5. John Kenneth Galbraith, *The New Industrial State* (New York: New American Library, 1967), p. 88.
6. Ralph Nader, Mark Green, and Joel Seligman, *Taming the Giant Corporation* (New York: Norton, 1976).
7. See Christopher Stone, *Where the Law Ends* (New York: Harper & Row, 1975).
8. Data for this historical analysis are from Nader et al., *Taming;* David Finn, *The Corporate Oligarch* (New York: Simon & Schuster, 1969); Ronald E. Seavoy, "The Public Service Origins of the American Business Corporation," *The Business History Review* 52 (Spring 1978): 30–60; Paul J. McNulty, "The Public Side of Private Enterprise: A Historical Perspective on American Business and Government," *Columbia Journal of World Business* 13 (Winter 1978): 122–130.
9. Stone, *Where the Law Ends,* pp. 19–20.
10. Nader et al., *Taming,* p. 37.

11. Ibid., p. 55.
12. Delaware Code Annotated, Title 8, Section 122 (Supplement, 1968), p. 15.
13. This discussion of Ralph Nader's proposals is based upon Nader et al., *Taming*.
14. Stone, *Where the Law Ends,* pp. 122–183.
15. Lewis D. Solomon, "Restructuring the Corporate Board of Directors: Fond Hope—Faint Promise?" *Michigan Law Review* 76 (March 1978): 581–610.
16. For a general discussion of this, see James S. Coleman, *Power and the Structure of Society* (New York: Norton, 1974).
17. Solomon, "Restructuring," p. 610.
18. Much of this discussion of whistle-blowing is based on Ralph Nader, Peter Petkas, and Kate Blackwell, eds., *Whistle Blowing* (New York: Bantam Books, 1972) and Kenneth D. Walters, "Your Employees' Right to Blow the Whistle," *Harvard Business Review* 53 (July–August 1975).
19. Based on Nader et al., *Whistle Blowing,* pp. 135–139.
20. Quoted in Nader et al., *Whistle Blowing,* p. 139.
21. Nader et al., *Whistle Blowing,* pp. 39–54.
22. "AAAS Committee: Details Legal Protection for Whistle-Blowing," *Footnotes* 8 (March 1980): 3. *Footnotes* is a publication of the American Sociological Association.
23. Occupational Safety and Health Act of 1979 (P.L. 91–596, Sec. 11c), Federal Water Pollution, Control Act Amendments of 1972 (P.L. 92–500, Sec. 507), Safe Drinking Water Act of 1974 (P.L. 93–523, Sec. 1450), Toxic Substances Control Act of 1976 (P.L. 94–569, Sec. 23), Resource Conservation and Recovery Act of 1976 (P.L. 94–580, Sec. 7001), Clean Air Act Amendments of 1977 (P.L. 95–95, Sec. 312), Federal Mine Safety and Health Act of 1977 (P.L. 95–164, Sec. 105 c), and Nuclear Regulatory Commission Authorization Act of 1978 (P.L. 95–601, Sec. 10).
24. The term *ombudsman* originated with a Swedish office created in 1809 to act as an intermediary between government and the public. It has since spread to other countries and to relations between nongovernmental organizations and their various publics.
25. Alex Inkeles, "Mobilizing Public Opinion," in Alex Inkeles, ed., *Soviet Society* (Boston: Houghton Mifflin, 1961).
26. Ibid., p. 222.
27. See Chapter 6 for a discussion of loyalty.
28. Quoted in Walters, "Your Employees," p. 27.
29. See, for example, Stanley Milgram, *Obedience to Authority* (New York: Harper Colophon, 1975).
30. Marshall B. Clinard, *Illegal Corporate Behavior* (Washington, D.C: U.S. Government Printing Office, 1979), p. 206.
31. Based upon Michael C. Jensen, "Watergate Donors Still Riding High," *The New York Times* Section 3, 24 August 1975, p. 1.
32. U.S. House of Representatives, 96th Congress, 1st Session, July 26, 1979, H.R. 4973.
33. P.L. 94–213.

34. Jeffrey H. Reiman, *The Rich Get Richer and the Poor Get Prison* (New York: Wiley, 1979), pp. 136–137.

35. Descriptions of the Park case are widely available, including S. Prakash Sethi and Robert N. Katz, "The Expanding Scope of Personal Criminal Liability of Corporate Executives—Some Implications of *United States* v. *Park,*" *Food Drug Cosmetic Law Journal* (December 1977): 544–570; William McVisk, "Toward a Rational Theory of Criminal Liability for the Corporate Executive," *The Journal of Criminal Law and Criminology* 69:1 (1978): 75–91.

36. Quoted in Sethi and Katz, "The Expanding Scope," p. 548.

37. Ibid.

38. Sethi and Katz, "The Expanding Scope," p. 570.

39. Tony McAdams and Robert C. Miljus, "Growing Criminal Liability of Executives," *Harvard Business Review* 55 (March–April 1977): 1.

40. *The New York Times,* Section F, 20 January 1980, p. 5.

41. Gilbert Geis, "Deterring Corporate Crime," in M. David Ermann and Richard J. Lundman, eds., *Corporate and Governmental Deviance* (New York, Oxford U.P., 1978), p. 286.

42. Opinion Research Corporation, "Anti-Business Sentiment Remains at an All-Time High," *ORC Public Opinion Index, Report to Management* 33 (End December 1975): 11.

43. That is, limited to the individuals punished. For a discussion of specific deterrence, see Jack Gibbs, *Crime, Punishment, and Deterrence* (New York: Elsevier, 1975), pp. 34–35.

44. Geis, "Deterring Corporate Crime." pp. 278–279.

45. For a fuller discussion, see Geis, "Deterring Corporate Crime," especially pp. 283–286.

46. Kenneth C. Elzinga and William Breit, *The Antitrust Penalties: A Study in Law and Economics* (New Haven: Yale U.P. 1976) pp. 30–33.

47. For example, see Ermann and Lundman, eds., *Corporate.*

BIBLIOGRAPHY

Ackerman, Robert W. "How Companies Respond to Social Demands." *Harvard Business Review* 51 (July–August 1973): 88–98.

———, and Raymond A. Bauer. *Corporate Social Performance: The Modern Dilemma.* Reston, VA: Reston Publishing Co., 1976.

Akers, Ronald A. "White Collar Crime: Crime in Business, Occupations, and Professions." In *Deviant Behavior: A Social Learning Approach.* Belmont, CA: Wadsworth, 1973. Pp. 177–192.

American Criminal Law Review 17 (Winter 1980). Symposium: White-Collar Crime. Part I — Investigation.

American Criminal Law Review 17 (Spring 1980). Symposium: White-Collar Crime. Part II — Sentencing.

Andrews, John Williams. "The U.S. vs. A&P: Battle of Titans." *Harper's Magazine* 201 (September 1950): 64–73.

Andrews, J. Scott. "Social Irresponsibility in Management." *Journal of Business Research* 5 (September 1977): 123–185.

Aubert, Vilhelm. "White-Collar Crime and Social Structure." *American Journal of Sociology* 58 (November 1952): 263–271. Rpt. in Geis, Gilbert, and Robert F. Meier, eds. *White-Collar Crime: Offenses in Business, Politics and the Professions.* New York: Free Press, 1977. Pp. 168–179.

Ball, Harry V. "The Use of Criminal Sanctions in the Enforcement of Economic Legislation: A Sociological View." *Stanford Law Review* 17 (January 1965): 197–223. Rpt. in Geis, Gilbert, and Robert F. Meier, eds. *White-Collar Crime: Offenses in Business, Politics and the Professions.* New York: Free Press, 1977. Pp. 318–336.

Bane, Charles A. *The Electrical Equipment Conspiracy: The Treble Damage Actions.* New York: Federal Legal Publications, 1973.

Barmash, Isadore, ed. *Great Business Disasters: Swindlers, Bunglers, and Frauds in American Industry.* Chicago: Playboy Press, 1972.

Barnet, Richard, and Ronald Mueller. *Global Reach.* New York: Simon & Schuster, 1975.

Barnet, Stephen R. "The FCC's Nonbattle Against Media Monopoly." *Columbia Journalism Review* 11 (January/February 1973): 43–50.

Baron, C. David; Douglas A. Johnson; D. Gerald Scarfoss; and Charles H. Smith. "Uncovering Corporate Irregularities: Are We Closing the Expecation Gap?" *The Journal of Accountancy* 144 (October 1977): 56–66.

Barry, Vincent E. *Moral Issues in Business.* Belmont, CA: Wadsworth, 1979.

Basche, James R., Jr. *Unusual Foreign Payments: A Survey of the Policies and Practices of U.S. Companies.* New York: The Conference Board, 1976.

Bauer, Raymond A., and Dan H. Fenn. *The Corporate Social Audit.* New York: Russell Sage Foundation, 1972.

Baumbart, Raymond, C. *An Honest Profit: What Businessmen Say About Ethics in Business.* New York: Holt, Rinehart and Winston, 1968.

———. "How Ethical Are Businessmen?" *Harvard Business Review* 39 (July/August 1961): 156–176.

Beauchamp, Tom L., and Norman E. Bowie, eds. *Ethical Theory and Business.* Englewood Cliffs, NJ: Prentice-Hall, 1979.

Bensman, Joseph, and Israel Gerger. "Crime and Punishment in the Factory: The Function of Deviance in Maintaining the Social System." *American Sociological Review* 28 (1963): 588–598.

Benston, George J. "An Appraisal of the Costs and Benefits of Government Required Disclosures: S.E.C. and F.T.C. Requirements." *Law and Contemporary Problems* 41 (Summer 1977): 30–62.

Bequai, August. *White-Collar Crime.* Lexington, MA: D. C. Heath and Company, 1978.

Bock, Robert H. "Modern Values and Corporate Social Responsibility." *MSU Business Topics* 28 (Spring 1980): 5–17.

Bower, Joseph L. "On the Amoral Organization." In Robin Morris, ed., *The Corporate Society.* New York: Wiley, 1974. Pp. 178–211.

Braithwaite, John. "Inegalitarian Consequences of Egalitarian Reforms to Control Corporate Crime." *Temple Law Quarterly,* in press.

———. "Transnational Corporations and Corruption: Towards Some International Solutions." *International Journal of the Sociology of Law* 7 (1979): 125–142.

Brandt, Michael T., and Ivan L. Preston. "The Federal Trade Commission's Use of Evidence to Determine Deception." *Journal of Marketing* 41 (January 1977): 54–62.

Breit, William, and Kenneth G. Elzinga. "The Instruments of Antitrust Enforcement." *Emory Law Journal* 23 (Fall 1974): 945–961.

Brenner, Steven, and Earl Molander. "Is the Ethics of Business Changing?" *Harvard Business Review* 55 (January/February 1977): 57–71.

Breyer, Stephen. "Analyzing Regulatory Failure: Mismatches, Less Restrictive Alternatives, and Reform." *Harvard Law Review* 92 (January 1979): 547–609.

Bruyn, Severyn T. *The Social Economy: People Transforming Modern Business.* New York: Wiley, 1977.

Burck, Gilbert. "The Hazards of Corporate Responsibility." *Fortune* 87 (June 1973): 114–117.

Burnhan, David. *The Role of the Media in Controlling Corruption.* New York: John Jay Press, 1976.

Burns, Thomas S. *Tales of ITT: An Insider's Report.* Boston: Houghton Mifflin, 1974.

Capitman, William G. *Panic in the Boardroom: How Business Got into This Mess and Some Suggestions for How to Get Out of It.* New York: Anchor Press, Doubleday, 1975.

Carroll, Archie B. "Managerial Ethics: A Post-Watergate View." *Business Horizons* 18 (April 1975): 75–80.

Carson, W. G. "The Conventionalization of Early Factory Crime." *International Journal of the Sociology of Law* 7 (1979): 37–60.

Chatou, Robert. *Corporate Financial Reporting: Public or Private Control?* New York: Free Press, 1975.

Child, John. *The Business Enterprise in Modern Industrial Society.* London: Collier-Macmillan Ltd., 1969.

Clabault, James M., and John F. Burton. *"Sherman Act Indictments, 1955–1965—A Legal and Economic Analysis.* New York: Federal Legal Publications, 1966.

Clarke, Thurston, and John J. Tigue, Jr. *Dirty Money: Swiss Banks, the Mafia, Money Laundering, and White-Collar Crime.* New York: Simon & Schuster, 1975.

Clinard, Marshall B. *The Black Market: A Study of White-Collar Crime.* New York: Rinehart & Co., 1952.

———. "Criminological Theories of Violations of Wartime Regulations." In Geis, Gilbert, and Robert F. Meier, eds., *White-Collar Crime: Offenses in Business, Politics and Professions.* New York: Free Press, 1977. Pp. 85–101.

———. *Illegal Corporate Behavior.* Washington, DC: U.S. Government Printing Office, October 1979.

———, and Peter C. Yeager. "Corporate Crime: Issues in Research." *Criminology* 16 (August 1978): 255–272.

———. *Corporate Crime.* New York: Free Press, 1980.

Coffee, John Collins, Jr. "Corporate Crime and Punishment: A Non-Chicago View of the Economics of Criminal Sanctions." *American Criminal Law Review* 17 (Spring 1980): 419–478.

Cohen, A. K. "The Concept of Criminal Organisation." *British Journal of Criminology* 17 (April 1977): 97–111.

Coleman, James S. *Power and the Structure of Society.* New York: Norton, 1974.

Coles, Robert, and Harry Huge. "Black Lung: Mining as a Way of Death." *The New Republic* 160 (January 1969): 395–402.

Committee on Environmental Controls. "Structuring Corporate Compliance Programs for Pollution Control." *The Business Lawyer* 35 (April 1980): 1459–1492.

Conklin, John E. *Illegal But Not Criminal: Business Crime in America.* Englewood Cliffs, NJ: Prentice-Hall, 1977.

———, and Erwin O. Smigel. "Norms and Attitudes Toward Business-Related Crime." Paper presented at the Symposium on Studies of Public Experience, Knowledge and Opinion of Crime and Justice. Washington, DC: Bureau of Social Science Research, 1972.

Conrad, Alfred F. "Reflections on Public Interest Directors." *Michigan Law Review* 75 (April/May 1977): 941–961.

Conyers, John, Jr. "Corporate and White-Collar Crime: A View by the Chairman of the House Subcommittee on Crime." *The American Criminal Law Review* 17 (Winter 1980): 287–300.

Cook, William W. *The Corporation Problem: The Public Phases of Corporations, Their Uses, Abuses, Benefits, Dangers, Wealth, and Power, with a Discussion of the Social, Industrial, Economic, and Political Questions to Which They Have Given Rise.* New York: Putnam's, 1893. Rpt. by Kraus Reprint Co., New York, 1969.

"Corporate Criminal Liability." *Northwestern University Law Review* 68 (November/December 1973); 870–892.

Council on Economic Priorities. *Buying Power.* New York: Council on Economic Priorities, Winter 1977–1978.

———. *Environmental Steel/Update '77.* New York: Council on Economic Priorities, September 1977.

———. *Guide to Corporations: A Social Perspective.* Chicago: Swallow Press, 1974.

———. *The Invisible Hand.* New York: Council on Economic Priorities, December 1976.

———. *Minding the Corporate Conscience.* New York: Council on Economic Priorities, Winter 1977–1978.

———. *Paper Profits: Pollution in the Pulp and Paper Industry.* New York: Council on Economic Priorities, 1971.

Cressey, Donald R. "Criminal Liability of Corporations." *McGill Law Review* 10 (1964): 142–157.

———. "Management, Fraud, Accounting Controls, and Criminological Theory." In Elliott, Robert K., and John J. Willingham, eds., *Management Fraud: Detection and Deterrence.* New York: Petrocelli Books, 1980. Pp. 117–147.

———, and James F. Short, Jr., eds. *Delinquency, Crime, and Society.* Chicago: U. of Chicago Press, 1976. Pp. 209–238.

Curnow, D. P. "Economic Crimes—A High Standard of Care." *Federal Bar Journal* 35 (Winter 1976): 21–33.

Davids, Leo. "Penology and Corporate Crime." *Journal of Criminal Law, Criminology and Police Science* 58 (1967): 524–531.

Denzin, Norman K. "Notes on the Criminogenic Hypotheseis: A Case Study of the American Liquor Industry." *American Sociological Review* 42 (December 1977): 905–520. Rpt. in Messinger, Sheldon L., and Egon Bittner, eds., *Criminology Review Yearbook.* Beverly Hills, CA: Sage, 1979: 537–552.

Dershowitz, Alan M. "Increasing Community Control over Corporate Crime: A Problem of the Law of Sanctions." *Yale Law Journal* 71 (September 1961): 280–306.

———. "Developments in the Law—Corporate Crime: Regulating Corporate Behaviors Through Criminal Sanctions." *Harvard Law Review* 92 (April 1979): 1227–1376.

Dirks, Raymond, and Leonard Gross. *The Great Wall Street Scandal.* New York: McGraw-Hill, 1974.

Dowie, Mark. "The Corporate Crime of the Century." *Mother Jones* 4 (November 1979): 23 ff.

―――. "Pinto Madness." *Mother Jones* 2 (September/October, 1977).

"Economic Crimes―The Proposed New Federal Criminal Code." *Business Lawyer* 27 (November 1971): 177–193.

Edelhertz, Herbert. *The Nature, Impact and Prosecution of White-Collar Crime.* Washington, DC: U.S. Department of Justice, Law Enforcement Assistance Administration, National Institute of Law Enforcement and Criminal Justice, 1970.

Edgerton, Henry W. "Corporate Criminal Responsibility." *Yale Law Journal* 36 (April 1927): 827–844.

Egan, John W. "The Internal Revenue Service and Corporate Slush Funds: Some Fifth Amendment Problems." *The Journal of Criminal Law and Criminology* 69 (1978): 59–74.

Eliasberg, Wladimir. "Corporation and Bribery." *Journal of Criminal Law* 42 (September/October 1951): 317–331.

Elkins, James R. "Corporations and the Criminal Law: An Uneasy Alliance." *Kentucky Law Journal* 65 (1976): 73–129.

Elliott, Robert K., and John J. Willingham, eds. *Management Fraud: Detection and Deterrence.* New York: Petrocelli Books, 1980.

Elzinga, Kenneth G., and William Breit. *The Antitrust Penalties: A Study in Law and Economics.* New Haven: Yale U. P., 1976.

Ermann, M. David, and Richard J. Lundman. "Corporate Crime: Unresolved Issues and Some Tentative Responses." Paper presented at annual meeting of the American Society on Criminology, Atlanta, November 1977.

―――. *Corporate Deviance.* New York: Holt, Rinehart and Winston, 1982.

―――. "Deviant Acts by Complex Organizations: Deviance and Social Control at the Organizational Level of Analysis." In Messinger, Sheldon L., and Egon Bittner, eds., *Criminology Review Yearbook.* Beverly Hills, CA: Sage, 1979. Pp. 524–536.

Ewing, David W. *Freedom Inside the Organization: Bringing Civil Liberties to the Workplace.* New York: McGraw-Hill, 1977.

Farberman, Harvey A. "A Criminogenic Market Structure: The Automobile Industry." *The Sociological Quarterly* 16 (Autumn 1975): 438–457.

Feifer, George. "Russia Shoots Its Business Crooks." *New York Times Magazine* (May 2, 1965). Pp. 32–33, 111–112.

Fien, C. C. "Corporate Responsibility Under Criminal Law: A Study of the Mens Rea." *Manitoba Law Review* 5 (1973): 422–439.

"First Amendment―Corporate Free Speech." *The Journal of Criminal Law and Criminology* 69 (Winter 1978): 544–552.

Fisse, Brent. "Responsibility, Prevention and Corporate Crime." *New Zealand University Law Review* 7 (1973): 256–283.

―――. "The Use of Publicity as a Criminal Sanction Against Business Corporations." *Melbourne University Law Review* 8 (June 1971): 107–150.

Flynn, John J. "Criminal Sanctions Under State and Federal Antitrust Laws." *Texas Law Review* 45 (October 1967): 1301–1346.

Francis, Joseph. "Criminal Responsibility of the Corporation." *Illinois Law Review* 18 (January 1924): 305–323.

Frey, James H. "Toward A Theory of the Deviance of Organizations." Paper presented at the annual meeting of the American Sociological Association. Chicago, September 1977.

Friedman, Howard M. *Criminal Prosecutions and Civil Injunctions Under the Securities and Commodities Laws—Federal and State.* Lexington, MA: Lexington Books, in press.

————. "Some Reflections on the Corporation as Criminal Defendant." *The Notre Dame Lawyer* 55 (December 1979): 173–202.

Fuller, John G. *The Gentleman Conspirators.* New York: Grove, 1962.

Garvey, George E. "The Sherman Act and the Vicious Will: Developing Standards for Criminal Intent in Sherman Act Prosecutions." *Catholic University Law Review* 29 (Winter 1980): 389–426.

Geis, Gilbert. "Deterring Corporate Crime." In Nader, Ralph, and Mark Green, eds., *Corporate Power in America.* New York: Viking, 1973. Rpt. in Ermann, M. David, and Richard J. Lundman, eds., *Corporate and Governmental Deviance.* New York: Oxford U. P., 1978. Pp. 278–296.

————. "Upperworld Crime." In Abraham S. Blumberg, ed., *Current Perspectives on Criminal Behavior.* New York: Knopf, 1974. Pp. 114–137.

————. "Criminal Penalties for Corporate Criminals." *Criminal Law Bulletin* 8 (June 1972): 377–392.

————. *White-Collar Criminal.* New York: Atherton, 1968.

————. "White-Collar Crime: The Heavy Electrical Equipment Antitrust Cases of 1961." In Clinard, Marshall B., and Richard Quinney, eds., *Criminal Behavior Systems: A Typology.* New York: Holt, Rinehart and Winston, 1967. Rpt. in Ermann, M. David, and Richard J. Lundman, eds., *Corporate and Governmental Deviance.* New York: Oxford U. P., 1978. Pp. 59–79.

————, and Robert F. Meier, eds., *White-Collar Crime.* New York: Free Press, 1977.

Glenn, Michael K. "The Crime of 'Pollution': The Role of Federal Water Pollution Criminal Sanctions." *American Criminal Law Review* 11 (Summer 1973): 835–882.

Goff, Colin H., and Charles E. Reasons. *Corporate Crime in Canada: A Critical Analysis of Anti-Combines Legislation.* Scarborough, Ontario: Prentice-Hall of Canada, 1978.

Goode, M. "Corporate Conspiracy: Problems of *Mens Rea* and the Parties to the Agreement." *Dalhousie Law Journal* 2 (February 1975): 121–456.

Goodwin, S. D. "Individual Liability of Agents for Corporate Crimes Under the Proposed Federal Criminal Code." *Vanderbilt Law Review* 31 (May 1980): 965–1016.

Gorring, Pam. "Multinationals or Mafia: Who Really Pushes Drugs?" In Wilson, Paul R., and John Braithwaite, eds., *Two Faces of Deviance.* St. Lucia, Queensland: University of Queensland Press, 1978.

Gouldner, Joseph C. *Monopoly: The Real Story of AT&T.* New York: Putman's, 1968.

Green, R. A. "Indications as to the Real Nature of The Criminal Responsibility of Corporations." *Victoria University of Wellington Law Review* 6 (February 1971): 85–97.

Griffith, Thomas. "Payoff Is Not 'Accepted Practice.'" *Fortune* 92 (August 1975): 122–125.

Gross, Edward. "Organizational Crime: A Theoretical Perspective." *Studies in Symbolic Interaction* 1 (1978): 55–85.

———. "Organizations As Criminal Actors." In Wilson, Paul R., and John Braithwaite, eds., *Two Faces of Deviance.* St. Lucia, Queensland: University of Queensland Press, 1978.

Grossfeld, Bernhard, and Werner Ebke. "Controlling the Modern Corporation: A Comparative View of Corporate Power in the United States and Europe." *The American Journal of Comparative Law* 26 (Summer 1978): 397–433.

Gunningham, Neil. *Pollution, Social Interest and the Law.* London: Martin Robertson, 1974.

Guzzardi, Walter, Jr. "An Unscandalized View of Those Bribes Abroad." *Fortune* 94 (July 1976): 118–121, 178–182.

Hadlick, Paul E. *Criminal Prosecution Under the Sherman Antitrust Act.* Washington, DC: Ramsdell, 1939.

Hartung, Frank E. "White-Collar Offenses in the Wholesale Meat Industry in Detroit." Rpt. in Geis, Gilbert, and Robert F. Meier, eds., *White-Collar Crime: Offenses in Business, Politics and the Professions.* New York: Free Press, 1977. Pp. 154–163.

Hawkins, Keith. "The Use of Discretion by Regulatory Officials: A Case Study on Environmental Pollution in the United Kingdom." Paper presented at conference sponsored by the Baldy Center for Law and Social Policy and Oxford Center for Socio-Legal Studies at State University of New York at Buffalo, June 2–3, 1980.

Hay, George A., and Daniel Kelley. "An Empirical Survey of Price Fixing Conspiracies." *Journal of Law and Economics* 17 (April 1974): 13–39.

Hazard, Leland. "Are Big Businessmen Crooks?" *The Atlantic* 208 (November 1961): 57–61.

Heilbroner, Robert, ed. *In the Name of Profit.* Garden City, NY: Doubleday, 1972.

———. "Rhetoric and Reality in the Struggle Between Business and the State." *Social Research* 35 (Autumn 1968): 401–425.

Herling, John. *The Great Price Conspiracy.* Washington, DC: Robert B. Luce, 1962.

Hopkins, Andrew. "Controlling Corporation Deviance." Paper presented at A.N.Z.A.A.S., January 1979.

———. The Anatomy of Corporate Crime." In Wilson, Paul R., and John Braithwaite, eds., *Two Faces of Deviance.* St. Lucia, Queensland: University of Queensland Press, 1978.

————. "Increasing Community Control Over Corporate Crime—A Problem of the Law of Sanctions." *Yale Law Journal* 71 (1961): 280–306.

Insight Team of *The Sunday Times* of London. *Suffer the Children: The Story of Thalidomide.* New York: Viking, 1979.

Iseman, Robert H. "The Criminal Responsibility of Corporate Officials for Pollution of the Environment." *Albany Law Review* 37 (1971): 61–96.

Jacoby, Neil H.; Peter Nehemkis; and Richard Eells. *Bribery and Extortion in World Business: A Study of Corporate Political Payments Abroad.* New York: MacMillan, 1977.

Johnston, Moria. *The Last Nine Minutes: The Story of Flight 981.* New York: Avon, 1978.

Joskow, Paul L., and Alvin K. Klevorick. "A Framework for Analyzing Predactory Pricing Policy." *The Yale Law Journal* 89 (December 1979): 213–270.

Kadish, Sanford H. "Some Observations on the Use of Criminal Sanctions in Enforcing Economic Regulations. *University of Chicago Law Review* 30 (Spring 1963): 423–449. Rpt. in Geis, Gilbert, and Meier, Robert F. eds., *White-Collar Crime: Offenses in Business, Politics and the Professions.* Free Press, 1979. Pp. 296–317.

Katona, George. *Price Control and Business.* Bloomington, IL: Principia Press, 1945.

Katz, Jack. "Cover-Up and Collective Integrity: On the Natural Antagonisms of Authority Internal and External to Organizations." *Social Problems* 25 (October 1977): 3–17.

————. "Plea Bargaining in the Prosecution of White-and Blue-Collar Crime." Paper Prepared for June Plea Bargaining Conference, French Lick, Indiana (May 1978). Pp. 1–44.

Kelman, Herbert C. "Some Reflections on Authority, Corruption, and Punishment: The Social-Psychological Context of Watergate." *Psychiatry* 39 (November 1976): 303–317.

Kobrin, Stephen J. "Comparison of Codes of Conduct for Multinational Corporations." *Journal of Business Research* 5 (December 1977): 311–23.

Kohlmeier, Louis M., Jr. *The Regulators: Watch-Dog Agencies and the Public Interest.* New York: Harper & Row, 1969.

Kramer, Ronald C. "Corporate Crime: An Organizational Perspective." Paper presented at the conference on "Trends and Problems in Research in Policy Dealing with Economic Crime." State University of New York, Potsdam, NY, February 1980.

————. "The Ford Pinto Homicide Prosecution: Criminological Questions and Issues Concerning the Control of Corporate Crime." Paper presented at the annual meeting of the American Society of Criminology, Philadelphia, November 1979.

Krasney, Martin, ed. *The Corporation and Society.* New York: Aspen Institute for Humanistic Studies, 1977.

Kreisberg, Louis. "Occupational Control Among Steel Distributors." *American Journal of Sociology* 61 (1956): 203–212.

Kriesberg, Simeon M. "Decisionmaking Models and the Control of Corporate Crime." *The Yale Law Journal* 85 (July 1976): 1091–1129.

Kugel, Yerachmiel, and Gladys W. Gruenberg. *International Payoffs: Dilemma for Business.* Lexington, MA: Lexington Books, 1977.

Lane, Robert E. *The Regulation of Businessmen: Social Conditions of Government Economic Control.* New Haven: Yale U.P., 1954.

——. "Why Businessmen Violate the Law." *The Journal of Criminal Law, Criminology, and Police Science* 44 (May/June 1953): 151–165.

Lawyer, John Q. "How to Conspire to Fix Prices." *Harvard Business Review* 41 (March/April 1966): 95–103.

Lazaroff, Daniel E. "The Legislative Attack on Oil Company Mergers: Dragon-Slaying or Search for a Scapegoat?" *University of Detroit Journal of Urban Law* 57 (Fall 1979): 41–53.

Ledogar, Robert J. *Hungry for Profits: U.S. Food and Drug Multinationals in Latin America.* New York: IDOC/North America, Inc., 1975.

Leigh, Leonard H. *The Criminal Liability of Corporations in English Law.* London: Weidenfeld & Nicolson, 1969.

Leonard, William N., and Marvin G. Weber. "Automakers and Dealers: A Study of Criminogenic Market Forces." *Law and Society Review* 4 (February 1970): 407–424.

Liazos, Alexander. "The Poverty of the Sociology of Deviance: Nuts, Sluts, and 'Preverts.' " *Social Problems* 20 (Summer 1972): 103–120.

Maltz, Michael D., and Stephen M. Pollock. "Analyzing Suspected Collusion Among Bidders." In Geis, Gilbert, and Ezra Stotland, eds., *White-Collar Crime: Theory and Research.* Beverly Hills, CA: Sage, 1980.

Margolis, Diane R. "Learning to Lie: Some Aspects of the Social Psychology of Corporate Crime." Unpublished manuscript, U. of Connecticut, 1978.

Marris, Robin. *The Corporate Society.* New York: Wiley, 1974.

Mason, Edward S., ed. *The Corporation in Modern Society.* Cambridge, MA: Harvard U.P., 1960.

Mathews, Arthur F. "Criminal Prosecutions Under the Federal Securities Laws and Related Statutes: The Nature and Development of SEC Criminal Cases." *George Washington Law Review* 39 (July 1971): 901–970.

McAdams, Tony, and Robert C. Miljus. "Growing Criminal Liability of Executives." *Harvard Business Review* 55 (March/April 1977): 1–4.

McCormick, Albert E., Jr. "Rule Enforcement and Moral Indignation: Some Observations on the Effects of Criminal Antitrust Convictions upon Societal Reaction Processes." *Social Problems* 25 (October 1977): 30–39.

McDermott, Beatrice S., and Freads A. Coleman. *Government Regulation of Business Including Antitrust: A Guide to Information Sources.* Detroit: Gale Research Company, 1967.

McDonald, B. "Criminality and the Canadian Anti-Combines Laws." *Alberta Law Review* 9 (1975): 67–95.

McGarity, Thomas O., and Sidney A. Shapiro. "The Trade Secret Status of Health and Safety Testing Information: Reforming Agency Disclosure Policies." *Harvard Law Review* 93 (March 1980): 837–888.

McLaughlin, Gerald T. "The Criminalization of Questionable Foreign Payments by Corporations: A Comparative Legal Systems Analysis." *Fordham Law Review* 46 (May 1978): 1071–1114.

McManis, Charles. "Questionable Corporate Payments Abroad: An Antitrust Approach." *The Yale Law Journal* 86 (December 1976): 215–257.

McVisk, William. "Toward a Rational Theory of Criminal Liability for the Corporate Executive." *The Journal of Criminal Law & Criminology* 69 (1978): 75–91.

Meier, Robert F. "Corporate Crime as Organizational Behavior." Paper prepared for presentation at annual meeting of the American Society of Criminology, Toronto, October/November 1975.

———, and James F. Short, Jr. "The Consequences of White-Collar Crime." Paper presented at colloquium on "A Research Agenda on White-Collar Crime," Washington, DC., August 21–22, 1980.

Miller, John S. "Deviance By Organizations: A Neglected Area." Paper prepared for presentation at annual meeting of Midwest Sociological Society, Minneapolis, MN, April 1977.

Miller, Samuel R. "Corporate Criminal Liability: A Principle Extended to Its Limits." *The Federal Bar Journal* 38 (Winter 1979): 49 ff.

Mills, C. Wright. *The Power Elite.* New York: Oxford U.P., 1956.

Molotch, Harvey, and Marilyn Lester. "Accidental News: The Great Oil Spill as Local Occurrence and National Event." *American Journal of Sociology* 81 (September 1975): 235–260. Rpt. in Ermann, M. David, and Richard J. Lundman, eds., *Corporate and Governmental Deviance.* New York: Oxford U.P., 1978. Pp. 297–308.

Mueller, Gerhard O. W. "*Mens Rea* and the Corporation: A Study of the Model Penal Code Position on Corporate Criminal Liability." *University of Pittsburgh Law Review* 19 (Fall 1957): 21–50.

Nader, Ralph. *Unsafe at Any Speed: The Designed-in Dangers of the American Automobile.* New York: Grossman Publishers, 1965.

———; Mark Green; and Joel Seligman. *Taming the Giant Corporation.* New York: Norton, 1976.

———; Peter J. Petkas; and Kate Blackwell, eds., *Whistle Blowing.* New York: Bantam Books, 1972.

Needleman, Martin L., and Carolyn Needleman. "Organizational Crime: Two Models of Criminogenesis." *The Sociological Quarterly* 20 (Autumn 1979): 517–28.

Neuman, Lawrence W., and Alexander Hicks. "Patterns of Antitrust Enforcement Activity: Corporate Crime and Social Change." Paper presented at the annual meeting of the American Sociological Association, August 1977.

Nickel, Herman. "The Corporation Haters." *Fortune* 101 (June 16, 1980): 126–136.

Ogren, Robert W. "The Ineffectiveness of the Criminal Sanction in Fraud and Corruption Cases: Losing the Battle Against White-Collar Crime." *American Criminal Law Review* 11 (Summer 1973): 959–988.

O'Keefe, Daniel F., Jr., and Marc H. Shapiro. "Personal Criminal Liability Under the Food, Drug and Cosmetic Act—The *Dotterweich* Doctrine." *Food, Drug, Cosmetic Law Journal* 30 (January 1975): 5–78.

O'Neal, F. Hodge. "Preventive Law: Tailoring the Corporate Form of Business to Ensure Fair Treatment of All." *Mississippi Law Journal* 49 (September 1978): 529–558.

Orland, Leonard. "Reflections on Corporate Crime: Law in Search of Theory and Scholarship." *American Criminal Law Review* 17 (Spring 1980): 501–520.

Pearce, Frank. *Crimes of the Powerful: Marxism, Crime, and Deviance.* London: Pluto Press, 1976.

Perez, Jacob. "Corporate Criminality: A Study of the One Thousand Largest Industrial Corporations in the U.S.A." Unpublished dissertation, University of Pennsylvania, 1978.

Pfeffer, Jeffrey. "Administrative Regulation and Licensing: Social Problem or Solution? *Social Problems* 21 (April 1974): 468–79

———, and Gerald R. Salancik. *The External Control of Organizations: A Resource Dependence Perspective.* New York: Harper & Row, 1978.

Phillips, David M. "Managerial Misuse of Property: The Synthesizing Thread in Corporate Doctrine." *Rutgers Law Review* 32 (July 1979): 186–236.

Posner, Richard A. "A Statistical Study of Antitrust Enforcement." *The Journal of Law and Economics* 13 (October 1970): 365–420.

———. "Optimal Sentences for White-Collar Criminals." *American Criminal Law Review* 17 (Spring 1980): 409–418.

Reasons, Charles E., and Colin H. Goff. "Corporate Crime: A Cross-National Analysis." In Geis, Gilbert, and Ezra Stotland, eds., *White-Collar Crime: Theory and Research.* Beverly Hills, CA: Sage, 1980.

Reiman, Jeffrey H. *The Rich Get Richer and the Poor Get Prison: Ideology, Class, and Criminal Justice.* New York: Wiley, 1979.

Reisman, Michael W. *Folded Lies: Bribery, Crusades, and Reforms.* New York: Free Press, 1979.

Reiss, Albert J., Jr., and Albert D. Biderman. *Data Sources on White-Collar Law-Breaking.* Washington, DC: Bureau of Social Science Research, 1980.

Ricchiute, David N. "Illegal Payments, Deception of Auditors, and Reports on Internal Control." *MSU Business Topics* 28 (Spring 1980): 57–62.

Robertson, Wyndham. "The Directors Work Up Too Late at Gulf." *Fortune* 93 (June 1976): 121 ff.

Roebuck, Julian, and Stanley C. Weeber. *Political Crime in the United States: Analyzing Crime by and against Government.* New York: Praeger, 1978.

Schrager, Laura Shill, and James F. Short, Jr. "Toward a Sociology of Organizational Crime." *Social Problems* 25 (1978): 407–419.

———. "How Serious a Crime? Perceptions of Organizational and Common Crimes." In Geis, Gilbert, and Ezra Stotland, eds., *White-Collar Crime: Theory and Research.* Beverly Hills, CA: Sage, 1980.

Securities and Exchange Commission. *Report of the Securities and Exchange Commission on Questionable and Illegal Corporate Payments and Practices.* Submitted to the Senate Committee on Banking, Housing and Urban Affairs, U.S. Senate, 94th Congress. Washington, DC: U.S. Government Printing Office, 1976.

Seidler, Lee, J.; Frederick Andrews; and Marc J. Epstein. *The Equity Funding Papers: The Anatomy of a Fraud.* Santa Barbara: Wiley, 1977.

Sethi, S. Prakash. *Up Against the Corporate Wall: Modern Corporations and Social Issues of the Seventies.* 3d ed. Englewood Cliffs, NJ: Prentice-Hall, 1977.

————, and Robert N. Katz. "The Expanding Scope of Personal Criminal Liability of Corporate Executives—Some Implications of *United States* v. *Park.*" *Food, Drug, Cosmetic Law Journal* 32 (December 1977): 544–70.

Shapiro, Susan. "Intelligence and the Vulnerabilities of Illegal Behavior: A Perspective on the Control of Securities of Violations." Paper presented at the annual meeting of the Society for the Study of Symbolic Interaction. New York, August 28, 1980.

————. "Thinking about White-Collar Crime: Matters of Conceptualization and Research." Unpublished paper, Yale University, March 1979.

Sherman, Lawrence W. "A Theoretical Strategy for Organizational Devinance." Unpublished paper, Criminal Justice Research Center, Albany, NY.

Shover, Neal. "The Criminalization of Corporate Behavior: Federal Surface Coal Mining." In Geis, Gilbert, and Ezra Stotland, eds., *White-Collar Crime: Theory and Research.* Beverly Hills, CA: Sage, 1980.

————. "Organizations and Interorganizational Fields as Criminogenic Behavior Settings: Notes on the Concept Organizational Crime." In Ermann, and Richard J. Lundman, eds., *Corporate and Governmental Deviance.* New York: Oxford U.P., 1978. Pp. 37–40.

Silk, Leonard S. *Ethics and Profits: The Crises of Confidence in American Business.* New York: Simon & Schuster, 1976.

Smith, Richard A. "The Incredible Electrical Conspiracy." *Fortune* 63 (April 1961): 132–137, and 63 (May 1961): 161–164. Reprinted in Smith, Richard Austin, *Corporation in Crises.* New York: Anchor/Doubleday, 1976.

Soble, Ronald L., and Robert E. Dallos. *The Impossible Dream: The Equity Funding Story.* New York: Putnam's, 1974.

Solomon, Kenneth L., and Hymar Muller. "Illegal Payments: Where the Auditor Stands." *The Journal of Accountancy* 143 (January 1977): 51 ff.

Solomon, Lewis D. "Restructuring the Corporate Board of Directors: Fond Hope—Faint Promise?" *Michigan Law Review* 76 (March 1978): 581–611.

Solomon, Stephen. "Corporate Lawyers Dilemma." *Fortune* 100 (November 5, 1979): 138 ff.

Sommer, A. A., Jr. "Corporate Governance: Its Impact on the Profession." *Journal of Accountancy* (July 1980): 52–60.

Sorensen, Theodore C. "Improper Payments Abroad: Perspectives and Proposals." *Foreign Affairs* 54 (July 1976): 719–33.

Southard, Samuel. *Ethics for Executives.* New York: Thomas Nelson, 1975.

Staw, Barry M., and Eugene Szwajkowski. "The Scarcity-Munificence Component of Organizational Environments and the Commission of Illegal Acts." *Administrative Science Quarterly* 20 (September 1975): 345–354.

Stone, Christopher D. "Controlling Corporate Misconduct." *The Public Interest* 48 (Summer 1977): 55–71. Rpt. in Messinger, Sheldon L., and Egon Bittner, eds., *Criminology Review Yearbook.* Beverly Hills, CA: Sage, 1979. Pp. 553–569.

———. "A Slap on the Wrist for the Kepone Mob." *Business and Society Review* 22 (Summer 1977): 4–11.

———. *Where the Law Ends: Social Control of Corporate Behavior.* New York: Harper & Row, 1975.

———. "Social Control of Corporate Behavior." *Where the Law Ends: Social Control of Corporate Behavior.* New York: Harper & Row, 1975. Pp. 35–50. Rpt. in Ermann, M. David, and Richard J. Lundman, eds., *Corporate and Governmental Deviance.* New York: Oxford U.P., 1978. Pp. 243–258.

Sutherland, Edwin H. "Crimes of Corporations." In Cohen, Albert; Alfred Linesmith; and Karl Schuessler, eds., *The Sutherland Papers.* Bloomington: Indiana U.P., 1956. Rpt. in Geis, Gilbert, and Robert F. Meier, eds., *White-Collar Crime: Offenses in Business, Politics and the Professions.* New York: Free Press, 1977. Pp. 71–84.

———. "Crime and Business." *Annals of the American Academy of Political and Social Science* 217 (September 1941): 112–118.

———. *White-Collar Crime.* New York: Holt, Rinehart and Winston, 1949.

———. "White-Collar Crime Is Organized Crime." *White-Collar Crime.* New York: Holt, Rinehart and Winston, 1961. Rpt. in Ermann M. David and Richard J. Lundman, eds., *Corporate and Governmental Deviance.* New York: Oxford U.P., 1978. Pp. 49–58.

———. "The White-Collar Criminal." In Vernon C. Branham and Samuel B. Kutash, eds., *Encyclopedia of Criminology.* New York: Philosophical Library, 1949.

———. "Corporate Crime and Social Structure." In Paul R. Wilson and John Braithwaite, eds., *Two Faces of Deviance.* St. Lucia, Queensland: University of Queensland Press, 1978.

Swigert, Victoria Lynn, and Ronald A. Farrell. "Definitional Processes Leading to the Homicide Indictment Against the Ford Motor Company." Unpublished paper, College of the Holy Cross, and State University of New York at Albany, 1979.

U.S. Congress. House Committee on the Judiciary. *White-Collar Crime.* Hearings before the Subcommittee on Crime of the Committee on the Judiciary, House of Representatives. Washington, DC: June 21, July 12 and 19, and December 1, 1978.

Vandivier, Kermit. "Why Should My Conscience Bother Me?" In Heilbroner, Robert, et al., eds., *In the Name of Profit.* New York: Doubleday, 1972. Pp. 3–31. Rpt. in Ermann, M. David, and Richard J. Lundman, eds., *Corporate and Governmental Deviance.* New York: Oxford U.P., 1978. Pp. 80–101.

Vanick, Charles. "Corporate Tax Study, 1976." *Congressional Record*, Proceedings and Debates of the 94th Congress, Second Session, Vol. 122, No. 151—Part III (October 1, 1976): H12327–H12331. Rpt. in Ermann, M. David, and Richard J. Lundman, eds., *Corporate and Governmental Deviance*. New York: Oxford U.P., 1978. Pp. 102–113.

Vaughan, Diane. "Crime Between Organizations: Implications for Victimology." In Geis, Gilbert, and Ezra Stotland, eds., *White-Collar Crime: Theory and Research*. Beverly Hills, CA: Sage, 1980.

Vogel, David. *Lobbying the Corporation: Citizen Challenges to Business Authority*. New York: Basic Books, 1978.

Wallace, Phyllis A., ed. *Equal Opportunity and the AT&T Case*. Cambridge, MA: The MIT Press, 1976.

Walton, Clarence C., and Frederick W. Cleveland, Jr. *Corporations on Trial: The Electrical Cases*. Belmont, CA: Wadsworth, 1964.

Waters, James A. "Catch 20.5: Corporate Morality as an Organizational Phenomenon." *Organizational Dynamics* 6 (Spring 1978): 3–19.

Watkins, Myron W. "Electrical Equipment Antitrust Cases—Their Implications for Government and Business." *University of Chicago Law Review* 29 (August 1961): 97–110.

Ways, Max. "Business Needs to Do a Better Job of Explaining." *Fortune* 86 (September 1972): 85–87, 192, 196, 198.

Weaver, Suzanne. *Decision to Prosecute: Organization and Public Policy in the Antitrust Division*. Cambridge, MA: The MIT Press, 1977.

Weiss, Elliott J. *The Corporate Watergate*. Washington, DC: Investor Responsibility Research Center, 1975.

Weissenberger, Glen. "Toward Precision in the Application of the Attorney-Client Privilege for Corporations." *Iowa Law Review* 65 (June 1980): 899–930.

Welsh, R. S. "The Criminal Liability of Corporations." *Law Quarterly Review* 62 (October 1946): 345–365.

Westin, Alan F., and Stephen Salisbury, eds. *Individual Rights in the Corporation: A Reader on Employee Rights*. New York: Pantheon Books, 1980.

———. "Trends and Problems in the Sociological Study of Crime." *Social Problems* 23 (June 1976): 526–534.

Wilson, P. R., and J. Braithwaite, J. eds. *Two Faces of Deviance: Crimes of the Powerless and the Powerful*. St. Lucia: University of Queensland Press, 1978.

Yoder, Stephen. "Criminal Sanctions for Corporate Illegality." *Journal of Criminal Law and Criminology* 69 (Spring 1978): 40–58.

Zald, Mayer N. "On the Social Control of Industries." *Social Forces* 57 (September 1978): 79–99.

INDEX OF NAMES

INDEX OF SUBJECTS